THE WEEK THAT OPENED FOREVER

THE WEEK
THAT OPENED
FOREVER

The Passion of Christ in a Different Voice

William J. O'Malley

ORBIS BOOKS

Maryknoll, New York 10545

ORBIS BOOKS
Maryknoll, New York 10545

Fathers and Brothers
MARYKNOLL™

Founded in 1970, Orbis Books endeavors to publish works that enlighten the mind, nourish the spirit, and challenge the conscience. The publishing arm of the Maryknoll Fathers and Brothers, Orbis seeks to explore the global dimensions of the Christian faith and mission, to invite dialogue with diverse cultures and religious traditions, and to serve the cause of reconciliation and peace. The books published reflect the views of their authors and do not represent the official position of the Maryknoll Society. To learn more about Maryknoll and Orbis Books, please visit our website at www.maryknollsociety.org.

Copyright © 2014 by William J. O'Malley

Published by Orbis Books, Box 302, Maryknoll, NY 10545-0302.

Manufactured in the United States of America
Design: Roberta Savage

Library of Congress Cataloging-in-Publication Data
O'Malley, William J.
    The week that opened forever : the passion of Christ in a different voice / William J. O'Malley.
       pages cm
    ISBN 978-1-62698-096-9 (pbk.)
1. Jesus Christ—Passion—Devotional literature. I. Title.
    BT431.3.O43 2014
    232.9'6--dc23
                                            2014005406

In gratitude for rebirth
to Jodi Olsen Kelly
and
the Jesuits of Seattle University

CONTENTS

Preface:
THE MUSTARD SEED

"Unless a grain of wheat fall into the ground and die. . . ."

—John 12:24

This book is about the week many of us—perhaps incautiously—claim is the most crucial in human history. Not only is it about the cross of Christ but about the crossroads of human destiny. It marks the final leap in human evolution when humans can finally legitimately aspire to a transhuman, divine life. It shatters whatever barriers blockade today from forever.

Moreover, it upends everything the Beast in us, the Freudian Id, wants to be true. (Christians claim what transpired this week, 2,000 years ago, is the ultimate manifestation of human fulfillment, its gut meaning. These eight days—Palm Sunday through Easter—establish the credibility of everything Jesus said or did in his lifetime. Any claim that he was, "of course, a fine moral teacher like Socrates or Mohammed or Gandhi but . . . ," is utterly foolish, since he claimed—unequivocally—that he was also God. If he was not, then he was either a madman or a charlatan. Holy Week claims to settle that question.

Kernelled in this week is the mustard seed. Like the tiny pretemporal singularity science says rocketed into the whole choreographed universe, Holy Week is the fiery core of all Christianity claims. The passion, death, and resurrection of this Jesus is not only the release of a consoling Spirit on a group of bickering religious communities. It is also the only answer Christians of all persuasions have found to make sense of suffering. Of life. Of anything.

Or so we say. Perhaps with little conviction. Or concern. Or comprehension.

When we think of success, happiness, meaning, this week's events do not merely challenge our present society's every dogmatic conviction. They strip away all their pretenses and expose materialism, consumerism, one-upmanship, "scoring," unbridled capitalism to be as desolate and deceptive as a Dali landscape, as directionless as the two hollow men of Beckett's *Waiting for Godot*.

On a bald knoll in an abandoned quarry outside the northwest Jerusalem gate, where felons were crucified and nearby rock-hewn tombs awaited the dead, the ultimate divine judgment on value took place. What our society cherishes and most longs for was judged—set against the Absolute Real—gilded garbage.

This week claims there is no renewal, no rebirth, no revolution or resolution without personal suffering and death, surmounted with dignity.

How could such a definitive determinant of human value and meaning fail to intrigue any honest inquirer? How could it defy our every previous conviction? Let me count the ways.

1. What Came Before

Jesus, the Nazareth carpenter, had already built up an impressive reputation, especially in the north, in Galilee, but also even in the south, around the Jerusalem capital. His fame there was a result of only a few trips, but the ruling hierarchy's network of spies and paid informers had kept steady watch on him for over two years, once he began attracting attention. He had a pack of misfit followers. Unlettered and mismatched malcontents are always a volatile stew, and the hills of Galilee often served as a staging area for revolt. Other Roman-occupied countries had been more pliant in the face of the inflexible demands of the invaders. Within a generation, other countries had adapted not only social customs and language but their heterogeneous gods, and found it a quite profitable loss, opening both markets and minds.

Alone of them all, Jews stood intransigent. Stiff-jawed resistance eroded any attempts to intrude pagan symbols into their Temple. Had not Judah the Maccabee, two hundred years before, defeated Greek and Syrian attempts to assimilate and homogenize them? Jews sneered at the comfortably familial Roman gods and the decadent culture with which the invaders were ever ready to corrupt the Jewish youth. They scorned even the face of the divine Emperor on the common coinage—though willing to exchange it for shekels, at a slight profit, in the Temple bank. The Hebrew hierarchy had achieved fragile peace and enjoyed the public's conviction that common folk would live more peacefully profitable lives if they left thinking to the priests.

Informants sent reports back to their handlers, not just from Jesus' home country around the Lake of Tiberias (which the natives still called Genesareth) but also from pagan towns along the Mediterranean coast in the west and from the far side of the Jordan River in the east. It was a small province to cover, a mere 150 miles from north to south, sixty miles at its widest. For the Romans—and to be truthful, for the religious establishment as well—the problem was not the area but the marrow-rooted convictions and bullheadedness of the occupants.

The reputation of Jesus bristled with unlikely stories, not merely fairly simple cures like skin diseases and nervous disorders but several cases, attested to even by reliable rabbis, of leprosy and outright madness. There were even reports that he had raised the dead. More than once. Such lessons would have called for little more than sneers from the sophisticated power brokers in the city, were it not for the simplicity of the people. And not just hill-country rubes but even among the more civilized common folk in the cities, who were always on the alert for some hint of a messiah to stand behind and sneer, someone to pitch the arrogant invaders back into the sea and govern them once more as a righteous king. The ignorant are always susceptible to superstition as a ready substitute for reasoned understanding of the transcendent, ready to accept mere sleight-of-hand for the miraculous. However, the holy Scriptures themselves did give a kind of credence to such naivete. Didn't the Sacred Books say with certainty the Unspeakably Holy One had no difficulty whatever summoning the endless savannah of the stars from sheer nothingness? Not to mention scorpions, sea monsters, and humans.

This Jesus was apparently a big, physically imposing, virile young man. He had attracted to himself at least a dozen hard-fisted types, ever-wary of a mountebank, plus one or two hot-headed Zealots apparently converted from revenge to nonviolent abrasion, even a tax-collecting collaborator. These were men in whom no pale rabbi could ignite a second thought, much less inspire practical men to shed everything to come out on the road with him. His relentless, bottomless patience and his stamina caring for the broken and outcast hours at a stretch testify to his charism as well. But the final testimony to his physical resilience comes at the end of his story, when his body was savaged with leaded whips, spiked to a cross, and yet he lasted—according to all reports—at least three hours in the searing sun. He gives the impression of being a man whose mere presence in a room causes silence. A man who rarely found need to raise his voice.

What follows, then, is pretty much what happened when God became one of us, when God decided he had to come and die to show us how he intended us to live.

Scholars from many disciplines agree he was born between 6 and 4 BCE. Few would focus more tightly than that. Since Luke suggests Jesus was "about thirty" at the time he began his work, one might safely place his adult entry on the public scene between 24 and 34 CE. More important, since these events are as much concerned with transtemporal realities as with realities of daily human life, accuracy is scarcely pivotal or even possible.

"Public scene" also seems a grandiose phrase for the journeys of a peasant preacher and his ragtag followers, men and women, around an insignificant province inhabited mostly by subsistence farmers, artisans, and tradesmen. Meanwhile, in the real world, the Roman Emperor Divine Augustus—who ruled most of the known world from Spain to Germany through Greece to Syria to Egypt and across all North Africa back to the Atlantic—died in the year 14 of our reckoning, causing a century of chaos as his family ruthlessly contended for what passed for power. In China, the Han Dynasty, which lasted four hundred golden years, was interrupted from 9 to 23 CE by a brief coup. Confucius had been dead nearly five hundred years and Socrates and the Buddha four hundred. In about 25 CE, as Jesus moved into manhood, humans first arrived on what is now called Pentecost Island in the South Pacific.

Yet in time, despite Confucius, Buddha, Socrates, and Augustus, the whole real world would situate itself in history based on the life of this obvious nobody.

Understandably, those who believed it important to go beyond his liberating message to the ways Jesus/God lived his own life embellished his arrival on Earth with stories underscoring his importance—a significance which remains unchanged despite any editorial exaggeration. The great Will Rogers suggested that, if preachers spent more time on our Savior's message and less figuring out his means of arrival and departure, we would all be a lot better off.

We may assume Jesus lived the life of an ordinary hill-country peasant boy, learning his rudimentary lessons in literacy and calculation from the local rabbi and from his foster father, who almost surely taught him carpentry skills. He learned the customs of his people and how to comport himself from his mother. Like every other boy, he must have assimilated the skills of confidence and compromise from dealing with his peers. Like every other adolescent, he must have wrestled with the two uniquely *human* questions: Who am I, and where do I fit in? There is no record of how he dealt with the seismic shift of puberty, though as a human he must have.

He began in Galilee, the northern third of Palestine whose people were scorned by Jerusalem city folk as coarse and ignorant. He hailed from a hill village called Nazareth, fifteen miles west of the great lake, which led even Nathaniel, the least guileful of them, to ask, "Can anything good come out of Nazareth?" (JN 1:46). One can only stand imaginatively helpless trying to ponder what transpired in the mind of a divine person, bereft of celestial insight, as God learned for the very first time. We know from the Gospels that he did grow in wisdom, and we know his insights baffled experts in the Law during one visit to the capital. The rest can be nothing but guesswork.

At "about thirty," he journeyed south—probably not for the first time—and gravitated toward a holy man called John and was baptized by him somewhere along the Jordan River that separated Palestine from its eastern pagan neighbors. It seems that at that time he met some of the men who would later become the Twelve: Philip, Andrew and his brother, Simon, all from the lake area of Galilee. He might well have even known some of them at home or met them on the long pilgrimage south, since it was unthinkable anyone would dare make the trip alone.

In that baptismal ritual, Jesus underwent the thunderous message that he was The Chosen One, the Messiah. But, as we can discern from the results, he realized the challenge was not a political one, to liberate his people from their most recent occupiers, but to free them fully—their souls, their very selves—from slavery to the fear of degradation by sin and annihilation at death.

Immediately, the Spirit of God "hurled" him into the Judean wilderness for over a month where he was tempted on precisely his conviction of being "*the* Son of God." Fortified by his long retreat, with renewed confidence in his call, he journeyed back north to Galilee and his hill country home around Lake Genesareth-Tiberias. There he gradually gathered the twelve novices to whom he would slowly reveal a totally new conception of human fulfillment. Over the next three years, they began to understand just enough to misunderstand almost completely.

In that first year, at his home base in Capernaum, a fishing village on the north side of the lake where Simon probably had a home, he spent a brief time trying to make an inroad on the sheerly this-world ideas his chosen Twelve had of the Messiah's mission.

Most of them had spent their lives on the lake, hauling in fish, hawking them to housewives or to processors for salting. It was a thin time for converts, the authority of a native son being both questionable and infuriating. Most of the time, he talked and the Twelve, and a few other men and women disciples tried to listen.

As in any school, perhaps one or two might even have understood, vaguely, and accepted, vaguely. It wasn't easy to learn, the way it is with a slipknot or which fish bite back. It took patience. On both sides. But what kept them with him was not the content of his preaching so much as the more-than-human power he exuded.

In the spring, according to John, Jesus brought them on their first of four 120-mile, home-and back treks to Jerusalem. Most probably, they took the longer route on the far side of the Jordan to avoid the mountainous route through Samaria, which also bristled with highway robbers and racial hatred. On that visit to the Holy City, John claims, Jesus drove the moneychangers from the Temple. But the three Synoptics [Gk: *synopsis*, "seen together," in parallel columns, i.e., Matthew, Mark, and Luke, whose outlines more or less agree and differ with John] seem to have the better claim, since such an outburst would hardly go unpunished, and such arrogance is more likely to have precipitated the end.

After the feast, they spread out into the southern district of Judea, and his disciples began speaking and baptizing, which caused an inevitable dispute with the Baptist's disciples. But John pacified them, ceding prominence to this greater prophet. On their way back north, they took the shorter route through Samaria, where Jesus met a woman of questionable reputation who nonetheless introduced him to some of her fellow villagers and gained respect for him.

Back north, he cured the son of a royal official at Capernaum, but when he tried to speak in his home synagogue in Nazareth, he enraged his former neighbors by what they judged his insolent assumption of authority. They tried to fling him off a cliff, but he merely walked through them, head high.

He finally summoned the Twelve to full-time service. He healed a madman and Peter's mother-in-law of a fever. With his dozen selected men and some women who traveled with them taking care of daily needs, he began a first tour of Galilee, preaching sermons which we know now are exemplified by the Sermon on the Mount (MT 5). In brief, it was a message no sage had ever suggested before: winning by losing.

He healed a leper, a paralyzed man, a man with a shriveled hand, a Roman centurion's servant. On trips across the Sea of Tiberias, Jesus calmed a storm and, in the pagan area eastward, healed a madman possessed by demons.

That second year, they ventured into the pagan territory that is now Syria and the Ten Cities of what is now Jordan. All along, Jesus had been harried by representatives of the various Hebrew sects: Pharisees (traditionalist, disciplinary, middle-class business-men, acceptable to common people); Sadducees (priestly, wealthy aristocrats, the majority of the ruling Sanhedrin, accommodating to the invaders); and Herodians (staunch defenders—self-serv-ingly—of the puppet "King of the Jews," the singularly corrupt Herod Antipas.) All these snappish parties were ready to suppress their mutual contempt to rid themselves of this uppity intruder.

The final journey in their third year was utterly foolhardy from the start. Every one of his obtuse inner circle agreed (which was rare) that it was worse than futile. Suicidal. Irrational. But Jesus insisted. He clung to some kind of plan they were unaware of. Nonetheless, even Thomas, the most hesitant of the lackluster dozen, finally huffed, "Oh, hell, let's do it, then. Let's go up to the city and die with him."

Instead, they ran. But that comes much later in the story. Like so many since, they had the best of intentions and yet, despite their evident flaws, they upended Western civilization and have long since been regarded as saints. Squarely in defiance of expectations.

Puzzling Moments

Journeys to Jerusalem

John, whose choice is most likely, has four journeys of Jesus to Jerusalem as an adult: first (2:23), at Passover in spring when he cleanses the Temple, faces down opposition by a claim to rebuild the true Temple in three days, meets an influential, sympathetic "leader," Nicodemus. Second (5:1), at "a Jewish festival," where he willfully defies the Sabbath to heal a man at the pool of Bethsaida and defends his authority. Third (7:14-10:39), after relatives appeal to him, he leaves and goes back to Judea, from Sukkoth in autumn, to Hanukkah, in late December. Once there, he defended himself against the authority of Moses, cured a blind man, causing some degree of upset to the authorities. Finally (12:12), John shows the final journey and the triumphal entry that the other three merge into one visit.

Which is the "truth"? Does it really matter?

There is a legitimate stylistic motive for conflating many journeys into a single trip. A metaphor of "life's journey" utilized by almost every society in history: Gilgamesh, Homer, Virgil, Dante, *Pilgrim's Progress,* Arthurian legends, *The Wizard of Oz, Lord of the Rings,* the *Star Wars* saga, *The Matrix, Life of Pi.* (Google, Campbell, Hero with a Thousand Faces.)

Mark's Messianic Secret

One instance of the ways in which a single journey can be not only a unifying plot device but also a revelatory insight is a choice that scholars have long called Mark's Messianic Secret, in which the writer tries to intrigue the reader just as a modern mystery writer might.

The focus of Mark's unique approach to the Gospel is in his question to Peter quoted above: "Who do you say I am?" (8:29). Right from the first verse, Mark has not kept the answer to that question from the reader: "This is the Good News about Jesus Christ, the *Son of God*" (1:1). But the question is what that *means.* The progression of Mark's Gospel is Jesus slowly establishing a basis on which he can ground his own answer to his own audience.

Imagine Jesus revealing his true identity from the start: "Who am I? I'm God!" Saying that to a crowd of Jews who bent over backwards to shield themselves from their polytheistic neighbors? Who daily insisted, "Hear O Israel, the Lord our God, the Lord is One"? Jesus would have been stoned on the spot, and there never would have been a Christian Gospel.

The secret that emerges—ever so gradually—throughout Mark's Gospel is that Jesus is an extraordinary person, capable of miraculous cures and speaking as no man had ever spoken. The first revelation comes at a miniclimax when Peter responds: "You are the Messiah" (8:29). But it reaches its fullest climax when Jesus is questioned by the high priest at the Jewish trial (14:61-62): "Are you the Messiah, the Son of the Blessed God?" And Jesus answers resolutely, "I am." He is not just the Messiah, but the unique Son of God. He even dares use the words no Jew would dare use: "I AM," the unspeakable name of Yahweh. At which, the high priest rips his garment at the shocking blasphemy. "We don't need any more witnesses! You heard his blasphemy." Finally, when it is all over, at Mark's quiet conclusion, the pagan Roman centurion at Jesus' death (15:39) answers that same question: "Truly, this man was the Son of God!"

It is arrogant to limit God to what we are capable of understanding.

The Plan: Building to the Kairos Moment

That final trip to Jerusalem defied reason. Against every prudent assessment, Jesus stubbornly clung to what he claimed was the "will of my Father." Which no one else grasped.

Unless, of course, one allowed the belief that irrational directives had been a focal feature of God's dealings with The People from the start. Starting over with the same two naked fools who had botched the original plan. Parenthood for aged, barren Abraham and Sarah. Stammering Moses sent to move immovable Pharaoh. Gideon the coward, David the slingshot stripling, Solomon the Corrupted Wise Man. The Lord has an intractable habit of defying expectations.

Rid yourself of the too-narrow metaphor of God's "Plan" as a meticulously plotted map, with every auxiliary road, topographical feature, and goat track carefully etched in, or like a constructed script for a play with every line foreordained by the Playwright. Such a limitation to "The Will of God" reduces the Liberator of energy, life, thought, and freedom to a puppeteer. Evolution gives solid evidence that our Creator is purposeful, but it also substantiates his penchant for what we might consider too much leeway for continued creativity. Rationalists fear a Playful God.

Many forget that spotless orthodoxy and rigid discipline are qualities and qualifications of Hebrew hierarchs and Roman imperators, not of the Jesus who we claim is the definitive embodiment of the will of God. The disciples and dinner companions he chose prove that.

We will have fewer problems with religion—that is, our connection with God—if we hesitate to remake him in our image. It should be clear to anyone over fifteen that life is much closer to a journey in which the exhilaration and meaning come not from arriving but from striving. The God who has been revealing himself to human souls from the beginning is demonstrably more into improvisation than into inflexible restraints. If so, then Jesus—true God and true Man—must have needed to make the same kinds of adjustments we do to unexpected intrusions.

Exorcisms and Miracles

Jesus was reported successful at exorcizing what everyone believed were demons. For those hesitant to accept such stories or even those who forthrightly reject them, it is surely possible these cases were forms of mental illness, which, of course, begs the question. An abrupt cure of schizophrenia is no less remarkable than disempowering an "evil spirit."

What's more, there has been documentary evidence up to the

present day of activities— levitation, manipulating objects without touching them, using unlearned languages—which defy explanation, and of a ritual that has actually released some victims. (See F. Scott Peck, *People of the Lie*, experiences of a renowned psychiatrist attendant on two actual modern exorcisms.)

A more down-to-earth defense. The core Christian doctrine is resurrection from death. We all stand and profess that belief every Sunday. Then it follows inescapably that we do believe in spiritual entities—souls—independent of their original bodies. It follows also that, existing incorporeally, they are now unlimited by time and space: they can be anywhere. And yet, belief in the risen Jesus of the Gospels accepts that such dead-and-reborn beings can reappear as convincingly as anyone still living. Moreover, common sense further demands that not every person who has died was good. Some were demonstrably evil. Therefore, it seems beyond denial that, if you believe in resurrection, you are stuck with also believing in "evil spirits," even though they are not as Hallowe'enish as All Hallows Eve nor ghastly as exorcism films. But we cannot consistently believe in resurrection and deny they *can* exist.

Historical or not, the Gospel exorcisms are noteworthy because they comment on the Message. The demons at Gerasa (MT 8:29) reacted to Jesus as no human did during his life: "What have you to do with us, O *Son of God?* Have you come here to torment us *before the time?*" These "demons" clearly express what all Christians now claim to believe. Not only did they fathom Jesus' genuine identity, but they also appear petulantly miffed that he is meddling with their domain before "the appointed time," the *kairos* moment, toward which Jesus' whole life is building.

On one occasion, the reports claim, at a wedding feast in the village of Cana, he transformed large jars of water into wine. And on these travels, he reportedly fed thousands—both of which events were at the very least a foretaste of what the miracle of the Eucharist would ultimately mean to the world. As for such a defiance of the laws of nature, skeptics readily accept that at one time utterly inert matter began to reproduce itself, vegetative life suddenly became able to feel and move about, and some descendant of brutish King Kong began to look about and ask "Why?" Nature has been violating itself for fourteen billion years.

What's more, if you can accept the literal transformation of bread and wine into Body and Blood, it should take little credulity to accept at least the symbolic value of the miracles of Cana and the multiplication of loaves.

As for raising the dead, all Christians, since the beginning, have wagered their lives that God can—and will—raise the dead. We are all tempted, however, to place limits of when and how God would be "allowed" to do that. To deny the *possibility* is as anti-intellectual as churchmen refusing to allow Galileo's sun-centered solar system, or Darwin's evolution of human beings from primates, or Hawkings's omnivorous black holes and Einstein's curved space.

To skeptics and to the hesitant, one might quote Benedict XVI: "If God does not also have power over matter, then he simply is not God."

Elements to Ponder

"Oh, I'm Nobody Special"

By all rational assessments, Jesus was a complete "nobody." No special education, no claim to admiration, merely his own confidence in his calling. What does that suggest to the rest of us nobodies? Like Adam and Eve, Abraham and Sarah, Noah, Moses, David, like Mary of Nazareth and Simon Bar Jonah, most of us have little claim as agents of the Most High God. What limitation does "lack of pedigree" impose on God?

God is like those wonder-filled people who haunt pawnshops and junkyards looking for "stuff" they can turn into something else. The kind of people who look at trash like bread mold or silicon chips and say, "I've got a hunch we could make something out of this." Be ready!

Clericalism

No matter how we try to diminish it, there is a harsh contrast between the ways of Jesus and the ways of the Hebrew hierarchy. Jesus was clearly as uncomfortable with them as with the Roman monarchy. "[The Pharisees] tie up heavy burdens, hard to bear, and lay them on the shoulders of others; but they themselves are unwilling to lift a finger to move them. They do all their deeds to be seen by others; for they make their phylacteries broad and their fringes long. They love to have the place of honor at banquets and the best seats in the synagogues, and to be greeted with respect in the marketplaces" (Mt 23:4-7) . . . . "You know that among the Gentiles those whom they recognize as their rulers lord it over them, and their great ones are tyrants over them. But it is not so among you; but whoever wishes to be great among you must be your servant, and whoever wishes to be first among you must be slave of all" (Mk 10:42-43). What lesson does that offer the genuine disciple?

"Prophets are not without honor, except in their hometown, and among their own kin, and in their own house" (Mk 6:4). That unlikeliest moralist, Francis Albert Sinatra said, "Show me a man without enemies and I'll show you a coward." What lesson does that offer the genuine disciple?

Even the Son of God himself was severely tempted to disbelieve his true importance and his ability to fulfill his mission. What lesson does that offer the genuine disciple?

The hand-picked inner Twelve were not chosen for their attainments or even for their promise. Any headhunter recruiting service would have rejected them to a man. Simon Peter was excitable, quick with rash promises, undependable when commitments became inconvenient. His brother, Andrew, seemed to tag along with his blustery brother. The other brothers, James and John, had delusions of grandeur and a mother more intrusive and insistent than a panhandler. Thomas, the twin, was an outright cynic, and Matthew (or Levi), a tax collector and Roman collaborator detested by everyone in town. Simon, the Zealot, was a "former" terrorist, and the rest were so colorless who could imagine one face? One candidate, however, showed great promise. Resourceful, self-confident, and with contacts in high places. Highly motivated, ambitious, and responsible: Judas Iscariot. What further evidence do we need that God's ways are not our ways? And yet this ragtag dirty dozen hapless losers changed the course of history.

We owe our existence to a God undaunted by the task of evolving a universe of countless billions of galaxies out of nothing—whose Son worked miracles with materials as unpromising as mud and spit; who can make a towering oak out of an acorn no larger than a marble; who, from two cells scarcely visible to the human eye, can make Shakespeare or Madame Curie.

What lesson does that offer the genuine disciple?

The Problem of Harmonizing the Gospel Versions

Those who remembered the stories of Jesus, those who gathered them, and the four who finally organized them into coherent sequences were not particularly interested in when or where Jesus said or did anything. Their interest was in what he said and did. Therefore, the six months leading up to the Crucial Week are a nightmare to wrestle into a single storyline—like trying to interlock the pieces of four different jigsaw puzzles.

Luke's Gospel focuses on a single journey to Jerusalem disproportionately: nine of twenty-four chapters. The journey itself is a parable of the Christian life before the ultimate challenge of suffering and death. Jesus sends the seventy-two disciples ("laypeople") out into the country on the far side of the Jordan for their first teaching experience, to arrange accommodations, and intrigue the audience for his coming. The journey is a lesson in discipleship. Almost a third of the material is unique to Luke and focuses on teaching over healing acts, the final preparation of his adherents for the challenge. He is trying to wrench their convictions of a worldly kingdom in precisely the opposite direction, one in which they will be sorely taxed to remain faithful. Part of that challenge is a second theme: the increasing opposition of those who hate and fear him—as they will his followers.

Matthew and *Mark* begin the single journey as Jesus leaves Galilee and the north behind and crosses the Jordan to avoid Samaria and travels gradually down the far side of the river, to Jericho, then to Bethany with the Lazarus family, then to the city. The "large crowds" Matthew claims "followed" him might be misleading. Like Jesus and his friends, those others were most likely themselves also on pilgrimage to Jerusalem for the great feast.

John has several journeys, and his Gospel could at least be read as spending most of Jesus' years of ministry in the capital. His version shows Jesus being confronted in the Temple at Hanukkah, in the winter of that final year, accused of blasphemy for making himself a god, and again nearly stoned. Then in early spring, he withdraws across the Jordan to Perea, where the other three Gospels show Jesus working his way south. From there, he is summoned back into Judea in hopes of saving Lazarus from death. That miracle proves the final straw, galvanizing his enemies' resolution to rid themselves of him. So, clearly in John's mind, Jesus awaits "the appointed time," the Passover, and he and his people retreat temporarily northward to a nowhere village called Ephraim.

In the following chapters based on itinerary described by Luke, I will tell the passion story in a voice that rises from within my soul, sprung from seven score of reading and praying the Scriptures, followed by a look inside puzzling moments and at graceful moments to ponder. I share this with you in a spirit of prayer.

2. The Final Journey: The School of Discipleship

"Yet today, tomorrow and the next day, I must be on my way, because it is impossible for a prophet to be killed outside of Jerusalem."—Luke 13:33

As soon as winter began taking its leave and the worst of the rains was over, Jesus' male relatives began a persistent effort to encourage him to take his carnival elsewhere. No one wanted him near his house because Jesus was never without his dozen layabouts. As soon as anyone knew where he was, they came swarming like locusts, with no regard to other people's goods and gardens. Since he'd proven unable or unwilling to let his relatives and neighbors profit from his so-called powers, wasn't it time he took his important ideas—and his mooches—up to the Big City where they belonged?

Jesus did, indeed, set his face unswervingly south, in order to be in Jerusalem by spring, which was still three months off, but it would be his final Passover. His reasons were inflexible, but quite contrary to his impatient relatives' motives. From now on, he was inexorably "on his way." To the destiny he was born for.

They set off for the shorter route, through Samaria, and since Luke reports Jesus later sent out seventy advance disciples—with no mention of names or sex—he probably left Galilee with many more than the chosen Twelve. As they advanced through the greening Valley of Jezreel toward the rocky spine of Samaria, Jesus sent scouts ahead to find accommodations, but they came back with the sour message that anyone on route to Jerusalem best find another way. Incensed, James and John, the Zebedee brothers, were keen to try their newfound skills and impale the villagers with lightning. Jesus dubbed them *Boanerges,* "Thunderboys," and gave them a tolerant smile.

So the large group turned eastward across the Jordan to join a caravan for the journey through pagan Perea. This route along the Jordan was twenty miles longer, hotter, and a steeper climb through a desolate wasteland of barren rock with twisted canyons and cliffs. They forded ordinarily placid streams now swollen with icy winter runoff. And, rather than hostile Samaritans, they had to be on lookout for mountain lions, bears, and brigands who lay in ambush along the trade routes.

On the way eastward, they were pestered by a Pharisee now and then, asking pesky questions, trying to trip Jesus up on differences with Moses, such as marriage and divorce, and about the galling subject of paying the Roman taxes, seducing him to incriminate himself irremediably. But Jesus continued, unfazed, warmly embracing and blessing children wherever they stopped, despite the Twelve's waspish resentment at the delay in their progress to greatness. Several men came forward, sincerely volunteering to join the pilgrimage, but Jesus made it painfully clear his call was more demanding than Elijah's call to Elisha. No personal benefits, no assurances, no turning back to tidy up their lives once they had put their hands to this plow. This group of his was aiming far beyond Jerusalem. Even those in the inner circle weren't clear on exactly what all that meant, but this Jesus radiated a kind of unearthly power and promise.

However, when the recruits understood the unmixed dedication a full involvement called for, some drifted homeward. One wealthy young man said he'd kept the commandments all his life, and Jesus loved him for that alone, but the boy found full commitment too costly. Yet there is no indication Jesus loved him less. Still, he used the moment to tell his people what a burden wealth is for those who want the Kingdom to the fullest—eternal life, true success, fulfillment. That left them bewildered, since it defied a belief in worldly goods as validation nearly as unbending as their belief in God.

As they entered pagan Perea, Jesus commissioned seventy disciples, as Moses had chosen seventy elders, and sent them as advance people, in pairs, to feel out likely places where he could pause and preach. This was their first trial run; he empowered these ordinary folk to speak and heal as he had been doing. He gave them the same instructions and powers Matthew reported he'd given the special Twelve (ch. 10) back in Galilee: to bless, to preach fearlessly, heal the sick, raise the dead, touch untouchables, dispossess demons. They were also to be utterly reliant on God, just as he himself was, not anxious about what they lacked. What's more, as testimony of their faith, they were to travel defenseless—without money, without a staff to ward off beasts or brigands. They need have no fear even of snakes and scorpions. What they were bringing to each village and house was peace. Whoever received one of his missioners would be receiving Jesus himself. Even prophets and kings had never been as gifted and privileged as the least of these plain men and women.

The newly empowered companions returned, jubilant with "their" success! "Teacher," they gushed, "even *demons* obey *us! Us!*" So Jesus was forced to remind them that it was his Father whose instruments they were.

More Pharisees had gotten wind of their success, and came out to take some of the starch out of their enthusiasm. When Jesus cast out demons, some sneered that it was a trick of the devil in him, luring their naive trust by pretending to yield to this fakir. Jesus scorned them and reminded them of the simple truth that "a house divided against itself is doomed." His message spurned pretense or miracles to provoke faith. His miracles were only in response to faith.

For whatever reason, a Pharisee invited him to dine and took pains to accuse Jesus of ignoring ritual washing, but Jesus retorted that his concern was not for the outside but the inside. And he used the occasion to make some imprudent— not to say suicidal—comments on the Pharisaic way, which Matthew (ch. 23) delivers with a vengeance. "Hypocrites who bind burdens on others that they themselves refuse . . . flaunting righteousness . . . blind guides . . . straining out gnats but swallowing camels . . . whitewashed graves thick with filth . . . assassins of prophets . . . tangled snakes . . . children of hell."

If Jesus had a minister of protocol, he would have been apoplectic.

And he predicted what his disciples could expect from those religious paragons: whipping, stoning, bloodshed, excommunication. All of which underlined the recklessness of his going up to the city. But his disciples still clung to the hope that the destiny that awaited him—and them—was his assumption of a fabulous kingship. Some of the slightly more astute, Judas perhaps, saw that the coming confrontation would give the final clarification of just what Jesus intended this new Kingdom to be.

Somewhere along their journey (although it is perplexing that only John records such a pivotal event), news came from their friend, Martha, a well-to-do woman they knew in Bethany, two miles southeast of the city. Her brother, Lazarus, a friend Jesus deeply loved, was deathly ill. But despite the urgency of the message, Jesus remained where he was, which puzzled a few of his companions. Then, after two days, he finally said, "All right. Let's go up to Jerusalem." Some of the more cautious said, "Teacher, at the Feast of Dedication last winter, they tried to stone you. Perhaps you might . . ." But Jesus said, "Our friend Lazarus is asleep. I'm going to wake him up." So they shrugged, "Well, if he's only asleep, no need for us to . . ." Jesus looked at them patiently. "Look," he said, "Lazarus is *dead.* I was waiting for that. So I could use this moment to root your feeble trust more deeply. So you can witness God's glory. Come."

They looked dumbly at one another. It was clear that, at least in his own mind, Jesus felt guided by a light from which they were excluded. But they weren't so benighted they didn't feel Jesus was struggling to open that light to them. So Thomas, the steadfast skeptic, heaved to his feet, and said, "All right. We might as well go up to Jerusalem and die with him. Let's go."

So they went. Loyally. Dumbly. They'd come this far. Where else could they go?

The town of Bethany sat on one of the undulant hills about a mile and a half over the Mount of Olives from Jerusalem. The family of Lazarus and his sisters, Martha and Mary, seems to have hosted Jesus—and at least the Twelve—whenever they were in Jerusalem. The personality of the brother is unclear, though more than once we are reminded how deep Jesus' affection was for him. The two sisters are more rough-sketched, Martha the forceful one, attentive to necessities, Mary, more soulful, susceptible, who clearly idolized the Teacher.

Martha went out to meet them as they approached the town. She was, understandably, ever so slightly reproachful of his delay. "Teacher, if you'd come sooner . . ." "But," Jesus asserted, "haven't I helped you see death is only temporary, Martha?" She confessed she did believe Lazarus would rise. On the last day. But . . . she even more firmly believed Jesus was the Messiah, the Son of God. She knew he was the way to resurrection. And their friend's reprieve from death. And even then she sensed he might have had a reason for his delay.

She gestured for him to stay where he was a moment, and she ran into the village to fetch Mary from among the friends who were sitting shiva, the week-long mourning, with them. Some even from Jerusalem. When Mary heard Jesus was waiting, she jumped up, and the sisters and mourners hurried with them to the high road. Jesus saw them approaching, all of them moaning and lamenting, and he seemed annoyed, almost angry. "Where have you put him?" he asked, and they led him to the tomb.

When they came to the rock grotto in a hillside, Jesus himself stood, silently weeping. Some said, "See how deeply he loved him." But a few sniffed, "He was only a few miles away. If he loved him so much, why didn't he come sooner? And do something. He does that kind of thing, doesn't he? Makes blind people see?"

Jesus looked at them, grim-faced. "Take away the stone," he said. Martha touched his sleeve. "Master," she said. "It's been four days. The smell." Jesus looked at her sadly. "Didn't I tell you? If you believe . . . ?"

So some men shouldered the stone aside.

Jesus raised his eyes and said quietly, "Father, I'm grateful you hear me. Always. Help them believe you sent me." Then he planted his feet, squared his shoulders and shouted, "Lazarus! Come out!"

Ever so slowly, into the dark doorway, the dead man hobbled, his ankles cumbered by the grave bindings, the kerchief easing down his bearded face.

"Untie him," Jesus said. "Set him free."

Everyone stood openmouthed. Dumbfounded. Incapable of accommodating what had happened. No ordinary man could have done this. Not the cleverest conjurer. And it wasn't evil. What could it be but the power of God within this man?

But one or two at the edge of the crowd slipped quietly away. To bring the story to their benefactors.

The Talmud deduces that the Sanhedrin, the great council, often met in the Hall of Hewn Stones, built into the north wall of the Temple, half inside, half out, with doors into the sanctuary and outside. The news from Bethany apparently called for a gathering of at least a quorum of the seventy-two lay and clerical members whose intrusions in public policy the Romans tolerated.

"And what are we going to do about this man?" they asked. "This is the last straw. Up and down the country. Around the outback.

Now right here under our noses. They're all running to him. What if he's here for Passover, when the city's crammed with pilgrims?"

"That's weeks away."

"More time to become an avalanche!"

"We have to act. Before the Romans get wind of it. The rabble will claim him king! The Romans will make us pay. Mark my word."

Caiphas, high priest at that time, was a realist, more expedient politician than churchman. Though the position was for life, the Roman governor often intervened, deposing and imposing, but this man had been cunning enough to hold on already for fifteen years. He stood and silenced them with a snarl, "Are you men blind? There's only one way. Eliminate him. One man dies instead of the whole nation." Which, without his realizing, was prophetic.

That moment galvanized their every intention to kill him.

No one needed a spy in that gathering to intuit their response to an affront as blatant as the rumor this Jesus had somehow contrived to resurrect a dead man. So Jesus and his followers withdrew from the city and made their way back to a nowhere town named Ephraim on the edge of the Judean outlands. That he went only twenty miles away suggests he had no intention to evade his death but only to control its time.

Orders went out that anyone who knew where this Jesus was hiding should report it to the authorities without fail.

Puzzling Moments

The Seventy

No matter when their sending occurred—or even if it didn't—these seventy (some manuscripts say seventy-two) are emblematic of the non-clerical Christians who now outnumber the clerics thirteen thousand to one. If we insist on the historical validity of this event, we're left to wonder why—after they return (Lk

10:17)—they're never mentioned again. Did Jesus disperse them back to Galilee? Did they continue on with him, posing a huge problem of lodging and feeding, especially for the long-suffering Lazarus family?

One's faith need suffer no threat if the occasion is a parable Luke invented to embody the truth that the task of active, aggressive apostleship is not limited to the few. Just as it is not a threat that Matthew, who wrote for Jews, may have invented the Magi to personify the truth that Jesus also came for wealthy, learned Gentiles. That is true, isn't it?

The Pharisees' Persistent Nastiness

Perhaps many longtime Christians have a too-childish image of the Gospel's Pharisees. It is beyond dispute that those who wrote the Gospels also were not objective about them, owing to the unyielding vicious treatment early Christian converts suffered from official Judaism and from their own Hebrew birth families. Like Hollywood treatment of Native Americans before it gained some perspective beyond the box office. It helps Christians to have a more mature grasp of the first disciples not as starry-eyed saints but as the bewildered, clumsy, faithless humans the evangelists were unafraid to show them to be. It could help in the process of seeing the Gospel conflicts of our own day in a more mature way, if we gave the "villains" a fairer treatment than the scowling, posturing, imperious caricatures of *Superstar*. It helps to try to puzzle out how the enemies of Christ, then and now, could justify their behavior—to themselves. Even Hitler had to make himself believe he was doing the right thing. As we will consider later, it helps if we also give Judas the same opportunity to become three-dimensional.

Think of other factions whose adherents became homicidally intolerant: the Inquisition, Bloody Mary and Elizabeth, the Salem Puritans, the KKK, Czarist and Stalinist pogroms, Armenia, the Gestapo, the Holocaust, the Great Leap Forward, Cambodia, Rwanda, Al Qaeda. Every one of those murderous rampages was impossible without the cooperation of ordinary men and women who would never even kill their neighbor's infuriating dog. But each was entirely— implacably—convinced to the roots of their souls that what they were doing was right. And in most cases, not merely right but fulfilling the irresistible will of an almighty Power.

O'Malley's Law: "You'll never go broke betting on *dumb*." And "dumb" has nothing at all to do with IQ or academic credentials. Oedipus was, by definition, the shrewdest man in Thebes. The one thing he lacked was *perspective*—and that brought "the wrath of the gods" down on the whole community. Both Communism and Utilitarian Capitalism have rational goals; each theory just ignores the unquantifiable value of a single human life. Almost all evil in the world has emerged from reductionism: the arrogant refusal ever to entertain the question: "Has it ever occurred to you that you might be *wrong*?" The great sin is certitude; the great educator is doubt. Any schooling system that fails to evoke in the young a breadth of perspective and a depth of compassion is merely a sorting agency for the Economy.

It is worth noting that, despite the blistering criticism of them in Matthew 23, Pharisees are mentioned in the *Passion* accounts only once each in Matthew and John and not at all in Mark and Luke. However, most of the "scribes" were likely Pharisees.

The Delay

It might seem heartless that, aware of the anguish of his friends, Jesus didn't hasten with all deliberate speed to ward off Lazarus's death. It is clear at least from the way the author of John treats the situation that Jesus delayed in order to make it inescapably clear Lazarus was dead. Unlike other occasions where Jesus revived someone recently dead (daughter of Jairus, son of the widow of

Nain), John—and Jesus—-make it clear that Lazarus has not been in a coma. He's been dead four days. Despite the heavy spices, he's begun to smell. Hebrew doctrine declared that after four days one could be sure the soul had left the body.

If it seems insensitive of Jesus, the reader has to remain aware that in a divine reality that transcends our intelligence, a billion years of suffering is as transient as the wake of a ship. That is very, very difficult to accept. But it is an inescapable corollary of our acceptance that God is God and not answerable to our expectations and priorities. A matter of perspective.

Again, the Miraculous

It is clearly possible to claim to be Christian with almost no genuine understanding of what that entails. One can forthrightly claim, "I accept Jesus Christ as my personal savior," without that incautious assertion including a readiness to be crucified for the ungrateful. It also can skirt or ignore or suppress the admission that no matter how brilliant we might be, our minds are beyond "impaired" in contrast to God's purview and understanding.

Although we already confronted the hesitation our sophistication poses for miracles, and although miracles call into question our grasp of what is possible, miracles also threaten our very belief in God. As Pope Benedict XVI wrote: "If God does *not* also have power over matter, then he simply is not God." In stark contrast, the learned astrophysicist Carl Sagan and microbiologist Richard Dawkins assert there cannot be any reality not established by empirical methods, by invincible evidence and argument. Such an uncompromising expectation also negates even the possibility of other such intangibles as love, integrity, trust, hope, a need for meaning. It also speaks with a dogmatism few popes have dared to use so unwaveringly.

The difference between the two claims pivots on what the individual will allow to be true. Is it impossible—intellectually indigestible—to accept there could be realities of which we are unaware, like a planet where the occupants do the right thing without compulsion or laws or fear? Could there be processes that we might be able to imagine or even describe occurring, but that we simply are presently unable to fathom—like a planet where every intelligent creature is hermaphroditic or telepathic or able to leap tall buildings at a single bound?

Is there anyone reading these pages unaware of the resistance/support of gravity? And yet, is there anyone who can explain *how*—and *why*—it *works*? Can anyone explain the seeming purposefulness of cosmology and evolution without an intelligence to program it? Can anyone explain how, as Sagan does, "one day, quite by accident, a molecule discovered a way to make crude copies of itself"? How does a brainless molecule "discover" anything? And once life had just "happened," what within it (or from outside this planet) enabled it to feel? And whence arose the impetus and wherewithal to ask "why?"

Is it "possible" that the most brilliant and objective mind could have looked at primeval planet Earth, covered with molten lava steaming into the atmosphere, and from that empirical evidence declare assuredly, "Well, of course, given enough time and random mutations, out of this *cauldron* will one day emerge a Shakespeare scratching the words 'To be, or not to be.' And someone, call him hypothetically 'Einstein,' will write 'e=mc2 'on a chalkboard."

How much gullibility does it take to accept now universally accepted scientific dogma that the entire breadth and power of the universe was first compacted into a dot smaller than a point in mathematics? That the breathtakingly vast and diverse universe was, before the instant of the Big Bang, compressed into a *singularity*: of infinite density and infinitesimal volume? How completely does it boggle the open mind to bow to the truth that within a zygote—a fertilized human ovum, visible only through a phase-contrast microscope with 10X objectives—are packed all the potentials that could ultimately become Michelangelo or Beethoven or Lincoln?

And those are just a few impossibilities we simply take for granted.

This crucial week celebrates a discovery more important than fire, the wheel, agriculture, a more radical opening than language and logic, more expansive to human meaning than the spherical sun-governed earth, printing, electricity, evolution, more life-changing than penicillin, relativity, electronics, and cold fusion.

This week calls on the justifiably proud human intellect to consider accepting the defeat of death. That there is a Reality beyond what our most exacting empirical sciences can verify. And two thousand years ago, a Divine Alien proved that a human being can be definitively dead and return to life. It is no longer a matter of hope but a matter of fact.

Elements to Ponder

Placebo Christianity

What follows is a worst-case scenario of the modern revision of the Apostles' Creed, the essence of what being Christian means. Few hold this pseudo-creed in its fullest impurity, but one is tempted to suspect far too many do.

I (sort of) believe in God, who started everything and lives way out there somewhere. It's impossible to communicate across such a huge gap and God's too busy with important things to concern himself over my trivial misdeeds. It's consoling, though, to remember somebody's "there for" me, like my fairy godperson, a heavenly 911 number.

I (sort of) believe in Jesus Christ, who preached we ought to be nice and help people (friends). Then he got crucified, died, and was buried. The third day (they say) he came back—which isn't really that important since I myself am not going to die for a long, long time. They say he de-scended into hell, but that's only a myth, so there's no such thing. He ascended into heaven, but till I get someplace, it's not really relevant. They say he'll come to judge the living and the dead, but that's also a myth. And a long, long way off even if it's true.

I believe in the Holy Spirit, which is a different name for the love human beings have for one another. I don't like the "holy" Catholic Church; it seems too mixed up for me. "Christian" is better, without "all those rules." I'd certainly want to be married in a church, have kids baptized and a church funeral. The real Church is more like a fellowship, nothing bossy like a "Kingdom." Communion of saints sounds good, but I'd honestly rather be called "loser" than "saint." I believe God forgives sins, even when we don't ask for it. And I believe in the resurrection of the dead and life everlasting, but again that's a long, long way off.

Amen.

In what ways does Jesus' handling of the apostles and disciples challenge that limp creed for the genuine disciple today?

Open-Mindedness

One mixed blessing about institutional churches is defined doc-trines. On the one hand, if we stand for everything, we stand for nothing. On the other, if doctrines become immutable, the insti-tution calcifies and begins to die. The first sign of a dying society is a new edition of the rules. The spirit no longer keeps the enter-prise alive. It requires the labor of mindless slaves.

If justice and mercy were the core of Christianity, every decent Jew, Muslim, and atheist would be Christian. At the very least we differ-entiate ourselves from other upright—even saintly—human beings like Albert Camus and Mohandas Gandhi in that we hold that Jesus Christ is the embodiment of God and the model of how God meant humans to be, that he died in order to rise and open immortality to us, that we show our belief in a worshiping and serving community.

Those who want to keep an open mind on such defining basics forget that the most open mind is an empty head. But any virtue, unchecked by its opposite, runs amok into a vice. Justice without mercy is vengeance, mercy without justice is rank sentimentality. Celibacy without passion is barren. Orthodoxy without flexibility and doubt is fascism. The personality of God revealed in cosmology and evolution shows beyond question a Creator discontent with stasis and relentlessly displaying a resolution to keep starting over, better this time. Without challenges to "what we've always believed," we would still be beating our chests and howling in caves.

The best any human enterprise can dare hope for is a high degree of probability, confidence with no *reasonable* doubt. Christians must never forget Christ was crucified by well-intentioned people for flagrant breach of orthodoxy. Anyone who definitively excludes—excommunicates—a member or group from the unitive Body of Christ ought to recollect beforehand that our Savior, his hand-picked apostles, and every original Christian were formally excommunicated from Judaism. That caveat should hold not only for official exclusions but all the more for personal condemnations. We must remember such rejections are saying, equivalently, "God damn you!" Few ought to feel empowered to sit on such a horrific jury.

In the parable of Wheat and Weeds (MT 13:24-30), the workers ask if they should gather the weeds the nasty neighbor has sowed. The Master answers, "In gathering the weeds you would uproot the wheat along with them. Let both of them grow together until the harvest time."

One more job, like being perfect, I'm willing to yield to God.

Resurrection

Are there reasons why we think of resurrection only at Easter and funerals? What effect would an honest acceptance of the inevitability and unpredictability of death have on the way we face waking up each morning? G. K. Chesterton suggested that, if Cinderella complained about having to leave the ball at midnight, her Fairy Godmother might have asked, "Sweetie, who said you could come to the ball in the first place?" Would we be less justified in complaining like Martha that God is slow on the uptake satisfying our prayers? Would worship, Eucharist, "thanks-giving" have a more vibrant meaning?

Freedom

The better to understand Jesus' humanity, think of him sending out these hardly "trained" disciples, to act in his name. It might help to understand Jesus' hesitation to recall the first time you let go of the bicycle seat, left a child in the kindergarten doorway, handed over the car keys for the first solo drive, kissed your daughter as she left on her first date.

It might also widen your perspective to realize that an omnipotent Father jeopardized his own freedom when he resolved to create human beings, the only species we know that's free not to fulfill its inner potential, free even to disrupt and overturn the *divine* will. At liberty to tell God, "Drop dead." And—unlike dinosaurs, mastodons, pterodactyls—he's allowed us to continue, despite our willfulness. How generous is that?

Baptismal Empowerment

Matthew 10 shows Jesus conferring extraordinary powers on the select Twelve. "And he called to him his twelve disciples and gave them authority over unclean spirits, to cast them out, and to heal every disease and every infirmity. . . . And preach as you go, saying, 'The kingdom of heaven is at hand.' Heal the sick, raise the dead, cleanse lepers, cast out demons." But Luke (10:19) says equivalently the same about the seventy "disciples": "I have given you authority to trample snakes and scorpions and overcome *all* the power of the Enemy; nothing will harm you."

Obviously, we can't take that deputizing literally—whether the first two groups were thus actually empowered or whether it was parabolic as walking on water embodies rising to challenges we think impossible. The nonordained can offer at least companionship to the sick. We can patiently try to lure those around us every day who are sunk in stultifying, fearful habits. We can ask a "leper" at work if he or she would like to get a cup of coffee. We can reach out to people bedeviled by fears of inadequacy, irrelevance, self-hatred. As soon as we turn on the TV we're nested in snakes and scorpions; can we take the good the media offer while being critical enough to escape its poisons?

Jesus said that, at the final judgment (MATTHEW 25), there is only one question. Not how much did you make, how many times was your name in the papers? Not a single question about sex or frequency of worship. The only matter of importance will be how *kind* we were.

"Let your light shine, so that they'll see the wonderful things you do and give glory to God in heaven" (MT 5:16). St. Irenaeus said, "The glory of God is humanity, fully alive." Fulfillment, success, happiness, "eternal life" emerges within us when we act like Christ: revivifying others.

Disappointments in Prayer

"If you ask anything in my name, I will do it" (JN 14:13). But that's simply not true. At least not as unconditionally true as it usually sounds. And any recourse to "maybe later" or "something even better" or "be careful what you pray for" just does not get God off the hook for not "coming through" on a promise. Not when he (rightfully) expects us to keep our marriage and religious vows. Reneging on such an open promise is just no fair.

And that is *precisely* true. It's *not fair*. Fairness has nothing to do with it!

But take that back a step, to Chesterton's Fairy Godmother. "Sweetie, who said you could come to the ball in the first place?"

If our Creator gave us the invitation to be here at all, is it quite fair on *our* part to spend too much time griping about the accommodations? ("They're closer to the band . . . her dress is so much grander . . . he has unfair looks . . . where are the waiters?") Even if the Host has said, "If there's anything I can bring you, just wave me down," it's at the very least bad manners to pout when he says, "I'm sorry. We don't have any left." Or if the Host had given you a voucher for a million dollars and you asked for "just a bit more?" The midnight curfew—death—should at least suggest that anyone intelligent ought to enjoy what you have while you still have it.

Still, the sense of being rebuffed is understandable. The saintly Job troubles God with his complaints for forty lugubrious chapters. But too many miss the whole point of Job's experience. Unlike the narrow orthodoxy of his so-called comforters, Job finally discovered—and yielded to—the truth that his disappointment with God's apparent capricious treatment was not a matter of *justice* but a feeling of betrayal of their *friendship.*

God "owed" Job *nothing.* But Job's *feelings* felt betrayed. And that is perfectly okay! Just as it is when a parent or spouse or friend—for reasons beyond our immediate understanding— betrays our unquestioning trust. Most times, we grit our teeth and go on trusting that friend, an act of faith based on all the *good times.*

That feeling is unavoidable, instinctual, not culpable. Just like any other emotion: anger, lust, envy, a craving for alcohol or drugs. It's a spontaneous "animal" response, like the uncritical cry an infant lets loose when you take away the pacifier. The emotion isn't blameworthy. Only our reaction to the stimulus is. Our attitude. Spend some time in a cancer hospital and see the different attitudes to the unwelcome "gift" of pain, loneliness, betrayal. Some react in anger, bullying even those who are just trying to help. Some implode into whining. But some respond to the unchangeable with a serenity that confounds the fortunate observer. Such trust in God— such willingness to forgive God—is astonishing. A miracle of friendship.

3. WAITING

"I came to cast fire upon the earth; and if only it were already kindled! I have a baptism to be baptized; and how eager I am until it is accomplished!"—LUKE 12:49-50

In Palestine, April is the greenest month. The world is coming back to life again. Trees quicken with buds and blossoms, farmers in the Jordan Valley begin the barley harvest. Passover was only a bit over a week away, so Jesus and his bread-mates gathered up their meager belongings and began the final trek down the valley from Ephraim to Jericho, where they would rest overnight and leave early next day. He wanted to be in Bethany tomorrow afternoon, long before Sabbath began at first starlight.

They trudged down the mountain side toward the Valley, hoping to join a southbound trade caravan or early pilgrimage for the feast. It was a mere ten miles from Ephraim to the river road and perhaps eight more to Jericho, a town rebuilt for centuries on top of at least twenty others. The rest of the journey was downhill most of the way as well, since the river dropped from three thousand feet above sea level at Lake Tiberias to eight hundred feet below sea level at Jericho, the lowest inhabited spot on earth.

The high road was fairly crowded. Camel caravans passed them by; pilgrims ahead of them stopped when there was shade, and the small Jesus group passed them. All day, strange faces filtered in and out of their party, usually disinterested, absorbed in their own next stop. A few fellow travelers seemed more attentive, some who had heard of this man's reputation. The Lazarus business and other stories. Others were even more alert, inquisitive, looking to trade any reports of his puzzling blend of openness and ambiguity to those in the capital who had more far-reaching interests. All men are highly sensitive to their own personal advancement.

As they walked, the enthusiasm of the Twelve began to grow. They felt the urgency and anticipation inside Jesus. They were all closing in on a climactic moment. Jesus sensed their expectation, and—for at least the third time in their years together—he knew he had to stifle their false hopes, try yet again to exorcize their stubborn misunderstanding, gird them for the trials.

"Listen to me. We're on our way up to Jerusalem. For the last time. Are you listening? The Temple people and the scholars are waiting for the Son of Man. They're going to arrest me. Do you understand? They'll give me to the Romans to mock me, torture me, flog me. They'll crucify me. But—I want you to remember this—on the third day, I will come back to life. Do you know what I'm saying? The Scriptures said it all along. The Messiah has to suffer."

And he moved on ahead of them, alone, certain it hadn't gotten through this time either.

They all nodded, hesitantly, stupidly, not grasping a word. They plodded on, heedless of the fact the Master had tried to smother their impregnable certitude. He was a superb human being, but the Scriptures didn't say *that* about the real Messiah at all. He'd be David come again. And what had Jesus ever done but kindness? Tweaked their pompous noses a bit? You don't get killed for that. Maybe they'd pick up cobblestones again. Just to hurt him. Scare him off again. But they'd be ready this time. Big men. Fearless. Or very close to it.

Impossible as it seems, the Zebedee brothers, James and John, aware of the narrowing delay between themselves and greatness, increased their pace and caught up with Jesus.

"Master," one said. "About this kingdom."

"We've been thinking about it a lot," the other chimed in.

"I could tell you were," Jesus said.

"It's going to happen soon, isn't it?"

Jesus took a deep breath. "Very soon."

"When it comes, you'll need men you can trust."

"Yes." Jesus frowned. "I trust . . . all of you."

"But like Moses. During the battle. With Aaron and Hur. To hold his arms up."

"You're husky young men. But I need more than that."

"Name it."

"I have a fierce initiation to face. Not just my body. My soul. And the cup. I have the bitterest cup to drink. Can you do that with me?"

They both said, unhesitating: "Yes. Right now."

"Ah, yes. You've got big hearts. You will face both. But not now. Later. When you finally understand. As for eminence . . . I have to let my Father take care of that."

The brothers lagged back, disappointed. And they hadn't been as far ahead of the others as they'd thought. The news trickled through the rest, and tempers began to simmer. Jesus turned and saw red faces and set jaws, so he stopped. They gathered around, breathing rancor.

"I keep hoping you'll understand. If you don't, who will? Look, ordinary soldiers wear scarlet cloaks. To scare people. And their rulers in their turn bark at them. Tyrants have to show off, to humble everybody else. Frighten them. Not you. If you want to be truly great, be happy to be humble, to serve. Remember the story of the Samaritan. You serve God by serving whoever you come upon in need. The Son of Man isn't here to command. He's here to serve. To give his life for those who are hostages to weakness and death. Do you understand me?"

They didn't have the conviction at the moment even to nod or say no.

Jericho is an oasis of palms. Even though the immediately surrounding plain is nearly waste and desolate, an underground spring called Elisha's Fountain made the town's soil bountiful, and its central location on the roads to Jerusalem made it a place of trade and hospitality. As they approached, the gates were crowded with pilgrims leaving on their way out for the Roman road to the city and caravans waiting to enter the town. A gift from God for beggars.

Some distance away from the gate and the raucous ebb and flow of animals and people, where even a strong voice was stifled, sat a veteran blind beggar named Bartimaeus. His dead eyes were closed against the dust. At the moment, he heard the voices of those nearest him, saying, "That's him! The miracle man. The one who raised that guy from the dead!"

Someone rasped, "Fool! Look at him. He's just an ordinary man."

"Don't call me fool. I was *there!*"

"Who?" Bartimaeus asked. "Who is it?"

"Jesus. Jesus Son of . . . somebody. They say he's the Messiah."

"I saw it. I was there! The dead guy's name was Lazer. Mazur!"

"And you're still a fool."

The blind beggar's heart jerked in his chest. A miracle man. With a voice long-trained to be heard, Bartimaeus yelled, "*Jesus!* Son of David! *Mercy!*"

Those around him jostled him and told him to shut his face. "He has no time for the likes of you!" Which made him all the more determined. "Jesus! Pity! Have mercy?"

Jesus stood still, and his men stopped around him. "Someone bring him over."

So two of them came and said, "Cheer up, old man. He's calling you." So Bartimaeus threw off his cloak and let them lead him to the road.

Jesus took his hand. "How can I help you, my friend?"

"Teacher," the blind man said, head bowed, "Help me to see again."

"Yes," Jesus said. "Your faith has saved you. See."

The blind man's eyelids snapped open. His face was radiant! "I can . . . I can . . . !"

Jesus rejoined his men on the road, and they moved again toward the village.

Bartimaeus grabbed his cloak, looked round. Not knowing what else to do, he ran after them. Shouting his thanks. Of course, the bystanders thought he was mad.

The news that some traveler—northerner from his accent—had cured a blind man ran like lightning through the crowd at the gates. By the time Jesus passed through and entered the tree-lined street everybody was jostling to get a look at him. One of the curious was a stubby little man named Zaccheus, insignificant in himself except that he was the local tax collector, so not only scorned but despised. His prodigious wealth was squeezed from the hard-earned shekels of his own neighbors—one-tenth of a grain crop, property, income; one-fifth of wine, fruit, olive oil, sales. He passed that on to the Roman occupiers. Mostly. He was, in very few words, a petty tyrant, collaborator, and extortionist. Beyond contempt. If that were not bad enough, he was the boss of a whole network of tax collectors. A petty prince among weasels.

The crowd was so dense and immovable, and Zaccheus so short, that he ran up and down behind the watchers, jumping, incapable of seeing anything but the backs of heads. When he tried to wedge through, they locked hips as if he weren't there. But his considerable wealth rested on his cunning, so he stopped and climbed a huge sycamore tree, with fat branches spreading out just above its squatty base. Dignity be damned.

Jesus looked up and saw this sweating, eager, piggy face peering through the broad leaves, and came to a dead standstill. Giggling, he said. "Zaccheus?"

The little monkey could only gibber and nod. "Uh . . . uh. . . ."

"Would you invite my friends and me to stay with you?"

Zaccheus bobbled his head "yes," and scrambled down from

his perch. He scurried over to Jesus, grinning and nodding like an excited puppy. He gestured through the crowd, like a waiter, and the people parted for Jesus and his men to pass through. Zaccheus danced after them, arching his furry brows left and right at his dumbfounded neighbors.

Not to be outdone, they sneered back. "He can't be the miracle worker! He'd know what a bottom-feeder that crook is!"

Zaccheus and his household couldn't do enough to welcome their dozen guests. The little man ordered his bewildered servants to rustle up a feast and ready every empty room to accommodate their guests overnight. He fluttered around Jesus, hardly able to contain himself. "Teacher," he gurgled, "I'm not a good man. Not worthy that you should enter under my roof."

Jesus smiled and touched the little man's elbow. "My friend, it's exactly because you say that so honestly which *makes* you worthy. You're the reason the Son of Man came."

As they reclined on couches around several tables, the Twelve were pop-eyed at the repast. Fancy bread, baked in various shapes, to be dipped in honey, oil, spices, and jams. Butter and hard cheese, fresh olives and fruit, and fish covered with almonds and sauces. And not just one wine but three, each better than the last. It was so sumptuous one might imagine Abraham, Isaac, and Jacob dropping by.

Zaccheus stood and raised his cup to Jesus. "Teacher, your kindness in befriending a man like me overwhelms me. Here and now, I promise you. I have too much. Half my possessions I'll give to the poor. If I've defrauded anyone, I'll reimburse them four times over."

Jesus stood and bent to embrace the little man. "Ah, Zaccheus! Today salvation has come to your house. You are true son of Abraham. I, your grateful guest, welcome you home!"

Next morning, very early, six days before Passover, they set out from Jericho with the pilgrims and caravans. It was only eighteen miles but steeply uphill all the way, a three-thousand-foot rise.

With breaks at the few water sources, it would take eight hours, and they couldn't be on the road after sundown when the Sabbath began.

The road to Bethany and Jerusalem ascends through narrow and rocky passes amid dry ravines and precipices. About five miles out of Jericho, travelers climb through Adumim, the Ascent of Blood. Some said the name came from its red rock walls; others claimed it was from the blood bandits had shed there.

As they walked, surrounded by other pilgrims, Jesus again told his story of the Samaritan who helped a man waylaid along this same stretch of road to Jericho, and other stories, old and new. He was like a man trying to pack the carryalls of his sons with supplies for a much longer journey. Because they were approaching Jerusalem and he felt the heat of their ambitions, he told the story of the nobleman who left his people with the task of carrying on his business, giving each his own amount of start-up money for the task, returning to praise those who had dared to take risks in carrying out his plans and castigating the timid, the overcautious, those of reserved faith. And he made them retell his other stories for one another as they climbed.

By early afternoon, they left the caravan on the highway and cut off on the road to Bethany. After they had washed away the road dust, they found themselves invited to pre-Sabbath dinner at the home of Simon, a wealthy man Jesus had likely cured of leprosy. Lazarus was an honored guest; Martha and Mary were there to help with the serving.

While the male guests were nibbling and chatting and the women were fussing efficiently about with serving dishes, Mary pushed through and knelt at the couch where Jesus reclined. Which no honorable young woman would dare to do. Without a word, she broke the seal on a long-necked bottle, and immediately the air blossomed with an intoxicating perfume. She spread the oil cautiously on Jesus' feet, then his head. Everyone watched, dumbfounded.

Only the wealthiest women could identify the woody aroma—cedar and hyacinth, lilac and lavender. It was spikenard. From the mountains of India. Hideously expensive. An ordinary man's wages for a whole year. When the men saw the women's reactions, they sensed a dramatic event. Not just an unacceptable intrusion by a young spinster. An insult to the host and all the guests? The girl was upset. Unbalanced.

Jesus simply smiled.

But Judas, their bursar, was infuriated. He leaned down his table and said to the others, "This is criminal! That perfume could be sold for a fortune and given to the poor." The others hadn't thought of that, but Judas was always a step ahead of the rest. They were prone to agree.

But Jesus hardly seemed to mind. He simply held up his hand to Judas, not angry, and he smiled at Mary, who was on the edge of tears. "Judas, don't fret so much. There'll be plenty of poor people left to be kind to after I'm gone. And Mary, don't be upset. You understand, don't you? A little. She's anointed me for my burial. She'll never be forgotten for that."

Their astonishment at Mary's intrusion had become complete bewilderment at what he'd said. His death? Conversations ceased completely. No one knew what to say. Gradually, out of an embarrassed need to distract themselves from the unthinkable, one here, one there offered some insubstantial statement. Purely surface. Anything deeper was just too confusing.

Gradually, because the Sabbath was quickly approaching, they began to take their leave.

Puzzling Moments

Apostolic Blindness

Is it even credible that the specially chosen Twelve could have been *so* obstinate in their inability to hear what Jesus was saying?

It does substantiate the evangelists' credibility that they didn't balk at showing the first pope and bishops so remarkably myopic that self-interest blinded them to what now seems so apparent to us. But that Mark and Matthew place this episode underscoring their refusal to consider his death *immediately* after the third prediction of his passion—Romans, flog, mock, crucify—actually strains that credibility. Could any group of men be that obtuse and manage to cope with daily life?

Then I started to think of the young men and women I've tried to teach apologetics and morality for fifty years. I hammered at them, daily, "Life does *not* play fair! . . . Lots of people work their hearts out and *never* 'make it'! . . . The real world is crammed with people who want to *out*-succeed you! . . . You have to learn to *think*! You can't get away with shoveling random drivel!" At the end of a full year of fulmination, they still believe, unchallengeably, that all the lights on the Yellow Brick Road to Emerald City will automatically turn green. At age thirty, no matter what, they'll be blissfully married and bringing home $90 grand.

Even a cursory grasp of church history reveals that no level of ordination precludes stubborn refusal to see and yield to the truth. Canon Law no. 98 flies against the facts when it declares—contrary to the experience of every parent and teacher in recorded history—that the ability to reason clicks on automatically at seven, just as puberty does in the early teens.

Those foolish enough to expect that all clerics have some irresistible "inner light" are blind themselves.

Prediction

Jesus was no fool. Even his less-than-clever followers found their eager anticipation of imminent elevation in status corroded by fear. The people whose power and prosperity Jesus' very existence threatened had spies everywhere. They all knew it. So did Jesus. Therefore, direct opposition wasn't a likelihood but a *guaranteed* obstacle in their immediate future. No transcendent insight need-ed to grasp that.

However, the specifics the writers include—Romans, mock, torture, flog, crucify—might well be an example of "backward reasoning," from their later knowledge, specifying a less detailed foresight Jesus actually did express before his death in less focused terms.

Atonement

Again, I have tried to soften, if not avoid, any attempt to justify Jesus' agony in terms of "ransom" or "retribution" by a detestable humanity to placate a God in rank contrast to the father of the prodigal son. I've tried to understand it without reference to the sole act of disobedience by a fictional couple and see it rather as God reaching out in an epically dramatic way to show not his implacable justice but his implacable love. A contrast perhaps not sufficiently rational for a Hellenic (diagnostic) rather than a He-brew (intuitive) mind. Jesus came to call, not condemn. To set us free from the fear that death annihilates us. To release those who choose to believe, not to free from a vindictive God but to free "hostages to weakness and death."

Mary of Bethany

Many Gospel women are named some form of "Miriam," the sis-ter of Moses who pushed his tarred basket into the Nile and di-rected Pharaoh's daughter to choose his own mother as his nurse. Also, there are two appearances of a woman who breaks into a meal to weep on Jesus' feet, one a woman known as a sinner, the other Mary of Bethany. Since a more prominent Mary (different from his mother) is Magdalene, out of whom Jesus had "cast seven devils," it has been overly tempting to cut down a confusing num-ber of cast members with the same name and fuse them all into Magdalene—who, as a result, is unjustifiably labeled a prostitute.

Some became even more reductionist and double her also with the woman caught in adultery (Jn 8:1-11).

There is little evidence to exclude two *different* events, one involving weeping and forgiveness of sins, the other an anointing very close to Passion Week as preparation for Jesus' burial. Each has a quite separate insight to convey. The first embodies Jesus' indiscriminate readiness to forgive: "Much has been forgiven her because she has loved much" (Lk 7:47). This moment in Bethany, on the other hand, like the story of the widow who gave up her entire paltry savings, exemplifies the indiscriminate response of the true believer. This perfume was a year's wages, close to $10,000, brought at outrageous effort from the mountains of India. Egregiously "wasteful"— but only in the same sense as a superbly qualified physician devoting her whole life to African AIDS orphans when she could have flourished on Park Avenue. "Wasteful" as monks who produce nothing more than jams and coffins and spend as much time praying every day as most people spend sleeping. "Wasteful" as Jesus dying for people who really don't care.

Judas

John is the only writer who specifies that Judas is the center of the discontent with Mary's ill-considered profligacy and the only one to focus his motive: "He was a thief." Further, the author hints Judas was in the *habit* of betraying his role as keeper of the purse. Unless (quite unlikely) he had other witnesses and proof of at least one other larcenous occasion, that judgment seems harsh and ill-founded.

The translation I chose was from Kurt Vonnegut, who confessed himself "a Christ-worshiping agnostic." He says "in translations jokes are commonly the first things to go." And Judas is here trying to "be more Catholic than the pope." But if the spikenard actually was worth the yearly wages of an ordinary man, today's $10,000 at minimum wage, who could help but gag at such a prodigious waste? Add to that: Judas was the keeper of the purse, the man Jesus routinely turned to when someone begged and said, "Judas, give him something," whom Jesus personally chose as treasurer—over Matthew, a professional, and the one who quite likely was the cleverest of the bunch. His irritation seems quite valid.

Perhaps whoever nailed that motive on Judas was also "more Catholic than the pope."

Elements to Ponder

Impregnable Certitude

Men like the Brothers Zebedee are still around. They preach and hope to practice a kind of "placebo Christianity." God is always "nice" to have around, like a Fairy Godfather. They claim, "I accept Jesus as my personal savior," which often sounds like a commercial for no-fault insurance. Their Christianity completely excises the crucifix. Or the same sort of people who say they've given up worship because "I don't get anything out of it." The reason for that is, almost surely, that they have their ungrateful fingers in their ears.

Oddly enough, for many people brought up to be "reserved," the greatest threat in being a genuine Christian is accessing exactly the intimidating kind of confidence the Thunderboys have in excess. Those who confuse humility with timidity, who hide behind the advice to act "like unprofitable servants." Such reductionism uses the same self-defensive blindness, as these two who were privileged to witness both the transfiguration and the agony in the Garden. They ignore that Christ told us to get up on the housetops and shout the good news of liberation from fear and death. To dare execution for their belief. Jesus was not executed for being reserved.

Blind Panhandlers

I confess, in embarrassing honesty, when some beggar asks me for loose change I almost always give it, but grimly, reluctantly. No problem in denying someone who shoves his cellphone into his pocket to put out his cup. Or who's dressed at least as well as I am. Why is it that I can't give him a quarter heartily? He's asking half the price of a single phone call, one-sixteenth of a Starbucks. Something unredeemed in me is sure I'm being "taken." Even though that is precisely the kind of gullibility the genuine Christian should have by second nature. (It goes diametrically against "first nature," the one we share with dogs guarding their bones.)

Would anyone freely choose to degrade him- or herself by standing on the street, hand out, to so many self-enclosed passersby? And Jesus' depiction of the Last Judgment shows clearly that such occasions are the norm by which our lives will finally be evaluated.

The Needle's Eye

Jesus seems aware of Zaccheus's name with no introduction. No reason given how, but he would also know he was notorious. And the little chiseler doesn't put the arm on Jesus. Jesus imposes himself—and his men—on him! This is like a cardinal-archbishop today asking for an invitation to a cookout at the Corleones, with other famous folks like Capone, Frank Nitti, Tony Soprano, Paulie Walnuts, Uncle Junior—not to mention the Mayflower Madam and her stable of ladies. What's more, Jesus offers his company long *before* the tax man has divested himself of ill-gotten gains. In fact, Jesus' kindness, his offer of friendship, causes the transformation.

Nor does Jesus show disappointment that the crook gives away "only" half of his legitimate earnings. The Zaccheus story meshes perfectly with the stories of the lost sheep, the lost coin, the prodigal son. Jesus accepted Zaccheus as unhesitatingly and unconditionally as he did the highwayman crucified with him. Jesus' kindness opens the way through the needle's eye.

Unlike the Zebedee brothers, Bartimaeus and Zaccheus swallow their pride and ask for help. AA members find freedom the same way: victory through surrender.

The Impractical Disciple

Just as Zaccheus with his profits, so Mary of Bethany with her perfume.

This Mary—in fact all the Marys, including his own mother—grasp Jesus, while males are reserved. This spikenard is an absurdly overvalued "thing," like sitting on either side of Jesus as he rules. Mary is profoundly grateful for what Jesus has done for her brother, and she intuits—at least to some degree—that Jesus will, in fact, be caught and punished, principally *because* of that. In giving Lazarus his life back, Jesus is going to sacrifice his own. But she also has, at least vaguely, accepted that Jesus is not intimidated by death. That he can defeat it.

Mary embodies the intuitive Hebrew mind, the "feminine" *yin* of the Confucian Tao, in contrast to the practical, rational Hellenic mind, the "masculine" yang. Her mind is innocent of the need to box in, to dominate, to control. She is by no means "dumb," not as the Twelve are. Unlike them, unlike even shrewd Judas, she has perspective. She is less complicated, more susceptible, less hesitant. On the other hand, she is obviously spirited and unchecked by taboos or etiquette—qualities also evident in such models of discipleship as Mary of Nazareth, Magdalene, women of the epistles who were leaders of house churches and deacons: Aphia, Prisca, Livia, Nympha, Phoebe, Thecla, Perpetua and Felicitas. Then Joan of Arc, Queen Isabella, Catherine of Siena, Harriet Tubman, Dorothy Day, Claire Booth Luce, Mother Teresa.

She is a focal figure in a week whose burden of truth is a "scandal to Jews, foolishness to pagans" (1 Cor 1:23).

Holy Week Timeline

There are as many timelines for the first four days of Holy Week as there are Scripture scholars. And far more than there were evangelists.

John has the purging of the Temple at the outset of Jesus' public life. But, at least editorially, it "works" far better toward the end: building to a climax, but most importantly, locking in a motive for his enemies to accelerate their resolve to kill him.

Mark *seems* to say Jesus and his friends entered the Temple, looked around, saw the chaos, and departed overnight to their friends in Bethany. Difficult to imagine one so dedicated surging to a peak of anger, walking two miles to their hosts', having a meal, a night's sleep, breakfast, the trip back, and retaining the same surge of revulsion. But Mark maintains they returned the next day (our Monday), and then Jesus drove out the hucksters.

Matthew and Luke *seem* to show Jesus losing his temper immediately on entering the Temple after the eruption of the palm-strewn ride down the Mount of Olives, driving them out, buoyed up by the affirmation of the crowd. On one hand, it's hard to imagine him seeing the chaotic desecration in his Father's house and just walking away; on the other, however, that's a very great deal of excitement for a single day. (And all the while one wonders where the Temple police were dallying.)

As for the next three days—before the carefully ordered events from Holy Thursday to the end—a timeline is nearly imperceptible. The cursing of the fig tree and cleansing of the Temple are enough for the other two Synoptics on Monday. But then Tuesday, it seems they have taken just about anything Jesus said or did that they hadn't used before and crammed it into that one day—with all four Gospels leaving Wednesday an uneventful day, presumably spent lazing around Bethany, praying, fidgeting.

Just before the final week, John shows the raising of Lazarus as one of the last provocations, the hierarchy's resolve to kill Jesus, the anointing at Bethany, Palm Sunday, and Jesus' predictions of his death and glorification. Then immediately he jumps to the Last Supper (our Thursday), which occupies *five* full chapters out of twenty-one.

In genuine dread of a scholar's reaction, I've surged ahead using "by-guess-and-by-golly," since the down-to-earth audience I envision would neither notice nor care.

And I'm also aware that, despite my singular deprivation of their divine inspiration, I'm doing exactly the same thing the evangelists did themselves.

4. The Incentive Moment

Yom Rishon (Sunday)

All Sabbath, they tried to rest, restlessly. They all wanted to engage their destinies. But if even God took a day off, who were they to outdo him? Even if that Sabbath were to be the Day of the End, they still dared not walk outside a town's limits more than a single mile. Bethany was twice that far from Jerusalem. So they waited.

Early next morning, they bade farewell for the day to their host and hostesses and set out climbing up the Mount of Olives, a series of hills across the Kidron ravine paralleling the prodigious eastern city wall. The high ridge of Olivet separated the city from the wilderness, running steeply beyond its hills down to the Jordan. They trudged up the hill, furred with thick pines, eucalyptus, figs, date palms. But mostly each side of the road was thicketed with squat-bodied olive trees, gnarled and bristled like ogres from a dream.

About a mile uphill, they saw Bethphage near the top. After such a short stretch, Jesus stopped and said, "We'll rest here a few minutes." He called two and gave them befuddling instructions. "Go into the village and just inside you'll see a donkey and her foal. Untie the colt and bring him here—carefully; he's never been ridden and will be skittish. If anyone says, 'What do you think you're doing,' just say, 'The Teacher needs it. He'll be sure to send him back.'"

So the two went and found things exactly as Jesus had said. Some people did ask what they were doing but seemed content with the cryptic reply. So they spread their two cloaks over the little burro's back and led him back to the main road. Jesus mounted him, and the party plodded on to the crest of the hill and stopped, amazed, looking across the valley. Even those who had been there before stood in awe of the panorama three hundred feet below them.

The majestic Holy City. Core of the Jewish identity. It spread along a great hill, rimmed by a monumental four-mile wall, spiked with turrets and towers, some places sixty feet high, circling the city. At intervals along the wall were massive gateways, and just inside each, a customs station where publicans collected taxes on all goods entering or leaving. The wall's blocks were eight-feet thick, some weighing one hundred tons, so huge they could have been laid only by angels.

At the city's heart, high on the cliff of Mount Moriah, reigned the gleaming, gold-crusted Temple, home of the Most High. At the Temple's far right edge hulked the Fortress Antonia, the humiliating presence of the invaders. Further left along its far wall, the Palace of King Herod, usurped on feast days by the Roman governor, who came south from his coastal headquarters to monitor the city's behavior. As far as they could see along the broad ravine below the Temple bluff, makeshift tents billowed, sheltering the influx of thousands of foreigners for the feast.

For centuries the hill to their left as they eased downward was a burial place, because the prophet Zechariah had predicted that on the Final Day, at the long-awaited return of Yahweh to Zion, the Messiah would begin the resurrection there: "On that day his feet shall stand on the Mount of Olives, which lies before Jerusalem on the east .... Then the Lord my God will come, and all the holy ones with him" (ZECH 14:4-5). People paid a high price for burial there in order to be first in line to heaven. Legend had it even Zechariah had heeded his own vision and was buried there himself.

As they began to descend, some noticed Jesus' eyes glittering with tears, and they heard him murmuring. "Jerusalem, Jerusalem!

If you—even you—only had ears to hear what peace means. Now it's too late. The days are coming! Your enemies will pile up earthworks against you, encircle you, overwhelm you. They will pull you crashing down. And your children with you! Not a stone left on a stone. You didn't recognize your God and make him welcome."

But those closest to him wanted to rouse his spirits at this climactic moment. So they shouted what was in their hearts, as Bartimaeus had shouted. "Hail, Son of David!"

As they began to push through the pilgrims along the hill path, men nudged one another, wondering what was going on. "You've heard of him. The Galilee miracle worker." And "Some say he's the one, the Messiah. And this is Olivet, no? Where he's supposed to . . ." Yet another, "You're sun sick. Messiah? Crazy." Someone chuckled, "You want to tell your grandchildren one day you were there the day the Messiah showed, and you didn't even *notice*?" and he joined in, "*Hosannah*, Son of David!"

Hardly any had ever heard of him, but the downtrodden ignite quickly at the least flicker of hope. All along the hairpin curves voices took it up, "Hail, King of the Jews! Hail, Son of David, our King! King of Israel!" Some reached up and pulled down branches from the trees, waving them in the air like flags. "Blessed! You come in the name of the Holy One!" They threw their cloaks and tatty shawls under the donkey's feet. This just might be the one. They'd have a relic of the day of days! The unlikely fulfillment of their lifelong fragile hope: "We have a king! Truly one of our own! A *nobody* king!"

A few Pharisees trotted along on foot next to the donkey and tugged at Jesus' sleeve. "Teacher," they huffed, "tell your people to stop this!"

Jesus brushed the tears from his cheeks, grinning. "If I silenced them," he threw his hand up toward the towering city wall, "those very stones would shout."

His Galileans pushed through the encroaching crowds of uncomprehending people who tried to touch this messenger from

God or at least capture a memory of his face as he sat on his docile mount. They crossed the Kidron stream and headed up to the double-arched Eastern Gate which opened directly into the Temple. More curious pilgrims. But also profiteers to capitalize on their every need, aware pilgrims always had forgotten something or hadn't brought enough of it, obsequious and ready to remedy their lack of foresight.

All the restrained energy of the Sabbath was let loose again this morning. A great many city-dwellers depended in large part on business the Temple and its feasts occasioned. Farmers set up booths with their wares: dried fish, cloth, combs. Pigeons to sacrifice for a woman's postpartum purification. Figs, slaves, spices. The gates swarmed with mountebanks, pickpockets and beggars, hawkers, peasants with blatting sheep. A raucous chorus haggling in Aramaic, Hebrew, Latin, and Greek. Sharp-eyed, red-caped soldiers cut a confident course through bodies and din.

The Jesus people edged their way through the double gate and turned left, into the vast eastern courtyard of the great Temple. And there they found the same chaos.

"He that has not seen the Temple of Herod has never known what beauty is."

The first Temple, Solomon's, had been razed to the ground in 586 BCE during the Babylonian captivity, rebuilt twenty-five years later under Cyrus the Persian. Then in 167 Antiochus IV, heir to the Seleucid Empire, erected a statue of Zeus in the Holy of Holies and triggered the successful Maccabean revolt. Finally, in 20 BCE, Herod the Great, father of the present Galilean puppet, brought the shrine to a jubilant fulfillment. For a time.

The Herodian Temple covered thirty-five acres, seven times as large as the Roman Forum, an area roughly twenty-five square modern city blocks. Its longer sides were two hundred feet short of a full mile. On either side of the towering central sanctuary, the Holy of Holies, were two enormous open courtyards, each boxed within cloisters, lined with three rows of Corinthian pillars, each pillar cut from a single block of marble thirty-seven feet high. The two esplanades were each 550 yards long, four hundred wide. On feasts, the two courtyards could accommodate a quarter million people.

In the center block of buildings was the Holy of Holies where the spirit of Yahweh dwelt among them, guarded by two outer courts, the outermost allowing purified Hebrew females, the middle one Hebrew males. But strict rules barred all others to the outer courts: those with skin diseases, the disabled, all non-Jews, women during their periods, any man after nonreproductive intercourse, shepherds and tax collectors, bastard sons of priests.

Priests, in white linen robes and tubular hats, scuttled everywhere, directing pilgrims and advising them what kinds of sacrifices were fitting for each need. But there was more. Around the huge open area, merchants hawked birds and bulls for mandated sacrifices. Moneylenders changed currency for travelers from far-off countries, shouting and waving at gullible pilgrims. Buyers and sellers yelled at one another, haggling over prices. Animals snorted and honked, birds screeched and squalled. The air was ammonia-sharp with the stink of urine and dung.

Jesus stood stock still. His jaw grinding, his eyes fierce with rage. "*No!*" he shouted, and his friends stared. Some customers turned for a moment and gave him an irritated glance, then turned back to their business. There were madmen everywhere you turned nowadays. At the side of one booth there was a hank of rope hanging from one of the awnings. Jesus tore it off and bunched it in his big fist.

"*Out!*" he bellowed and whipped the handful of rope around his head, moving into the crowd and scattering cringing customers. He reached a flimsy counter and glared at the wide-eyed official Temple moneychanger. He upended the table and sent the coin boxes and their contents flying. A few dropped to their knees and scrambled to pick up at least a few coins. He pushed past and hurled wooden cages crammed with fluttering screaming birds into the air. He turned and began whipping bleating sheep, stampeding them into other booths and sending the wares flying in every direction.

The chaos spread like mountain fire. Fleeing customers knocked one another over, crashing into other businesses and unleashing their animals and purchasers. That whole area of the enormous plaza erupted in a honking, squealing, shrieking pandemonium. People and animals pushed in panic into the colonnades and across the esplanade.

Jesus stopped, shellacked in sweat, and cried out like a man mortally wounded: "This is a house of *prayer*!" He cried. "For all nations! You've made it a den of *thieves*!"

He stood alone in the wreckage he had caused, hands on his knees, heaving for breath.

A couple of his men came and grasped him by the arms. Quietly, they led him docilely toward the gate and outside, where they all slowly left to climb the mount back to Bethany.

Of all them, one wonders if the whole event might have given the greatest shock to Judas. This business with "King of the Jews" and the violence in the Temple were worlds distant from the Jesus they knew and from the Kingdom Jesus had converted him to. So very much more like a triumphal, Davidic, combative new world.

But the officials found the fury of this upstart quite to their liking.

Puzzling Questions

Numbers

Matthew writes, "*All the city* was stirred." Tacitus set that number as half a million. Mark: "those who went before him and those who followed were shouting"; Luke: "the whole multitude of the disciples." The same is true of the riotous Temple scene. The Temple was one of the hugest buildings in the world. Almost a week before the feast, how many were there?

In trying to focus a composition of place, imagine a director sketching out needs for the scene. Some must have had unlimited budgets for walk-ons, animals, props, costumes. Just one Temple courtyard was the length of five football fields, the width of eight. If Jesus had created a ruckus in such a space, how many would notice anything more than "a big fuss over yonder"?

Certainly there were thousands camped in the valley, but hard to guess in the twenty-mile valley how many could have been focused on Jesus. Unlike films, it was not like a ticker-tape parade. More likely hundreds, although all along Luke has given the impression the number of "disciples" has been growing.

Their tumultuous reaction? We all know how little it takes to make a crowd react. A revival meeting? A rock concert? The Super Bowl? The Temple cheerleaders will get the exact opposite reaction from the same crowd next Friday morning.

Son of David! / King of the Jews!

Those cries intentionally give both scenes a messianic tone, although neither is quite what Zechariah (or film directors) envisioned. The following Friday is evidence enough of the shallowness of their appreciation. Even the disciples (except maybe Judas) seem to have forgotten the Sermon on the Mount. This was much more *like* it!

Earlier, after the Bread of Life discourse, Jesus said, "Unless you eat the flesh of the Son of Man and drink his blood, you have no life in you" (Jn 6:53). After years of reflection, we now see Jesus was a sign of contradiction, but at that time many worthy adherents walked away. The Twelve—and probably not only they—stayed. The question why they stayed is as open to the imagination as why they followed him in the first place.

But the titles, ironically, offered the Powers-That-Be precisely the handle they needed when they petitioned the governor for the death penalty.

Prediction

Zechariah 9:9-10: "Rejoice greatly, O Daughter of Zion! Shout, Daughter of Jerusalem! See, your king comes to you, righteous and having salvation, gentle and riding on a donkey, on a colt, the foal of a donkey. I will take away the chariots from Ephraim and the warhorses from Jerusalem, and the battle bow will be broken. He will proclaim peace to the nations. His rule will extend from sea to sea and from the River to the ends of the earth."

Rather than lean too heavily on a vision of time-traveling back to ancient Israel from these present events, it is quite possible to accept that the evangelists (and the evolving communities they served) were "embellishing" the event (like the Bethlehem angels) by recognizing resonances to Zechariah 9:9, Daniel 9:25-26, and Psalm 118:21-29. And the "predictions" became more exact by hindsight. The writers didn't necessarily fabricate the events so much as use previous descriptions of the Messiah to educe the "really real" of who Jesus was and is.

The people the Gospels were written for firmly *believed* that, no matter appearances or what we think possible, "the time of your visitation (*kairos*) is now" (Lk 19:44).

Judas Iscariot

In these pages, I take my cue from Dorothy Sayers's fine series of radio plays for the BBC collected as *The Man Born to Be King*. She is not a Scripture scholar, but she has an intriguing insight into the puzzling motivation behind Judas's startling turnabout— after three intense years with this charismatic teacher. She writes:

> One thing is certain: he cannot have been the creeping, crawling, patently worthless villain that some simple-mind-

ed people would like to make out; that would be to cast too grave a slur upon the brains or character of Jesus. To choose an obvious crook as one's follower, in ignorance of what he was like, would be the act of a fool; and Jesus of Nazareth was no fool.

Unlike the fishermen and Matthew, we have no clue to his calling. Her theory is that Judas, like the Simon the writers identify as a Zealot, had been a "freedom fighter," like a member of the IRA, provoking the Romans and fomenting armed resistance. Some have written along those lines that "Iscariot" is not an identification by his village, "of Kerioth," but rather association with the *Sicarii* (dagger men) who randomly knifed soldiers and caused havoc in crowds. Perhaps Sayers is right about his rebelliousness, but men with that explicit designation (*sicarius*) weren't around until much later. However, why should her theory have less potential than a scholar's imaginative explanation?

Sayers argues that Jesus had *really* converted Judas. As thorough an inversion as the effect of the risen Jesus on Saul on his way to Damascus to persecute Christians. Completely. But these two first-day events were too much for Judas's trust in Jesus. The other disciples were exhilarated. The reception on the way into Jerusalem was clear evidence their selfish ideas of this Kingdom were *right* all along. It's started! The royal treatment! And Jesus *didn't* object, much less reject. Even with the Pharisees along the way warning him he was crossing the line. A thoughtful man like Judas could have been a countercultural idealist, like Che Guevara. And at this jarring change in tactics, he might have wondered whether Jesus still meant what he'd said all along, that the king must be a servant. All that talk about the poor, the outcasts, the downtrodden? The hideous waste of the spikenard? Then the raw violence in the Temple! Peace? Was this "the other cheek"? Was Jesus finally the victim of too much success?

Sayers suggests Judas betrayed Jesus to save him from himself. It was an act of love.

The Plan

All the writers are at pains to show how obviously well planned this week is. Whether the Hebrew prophets actually foresaw it as clearly as we might imagine is somewhat irrelevant. The details show a consistent *intention*. Jesus is clearly inviting attention and courting arrest. He is blatantly taunting the hierarchy to a point they can simply no longer restrain their complete rejection of him and stirring up an audience to witness what he intends to cause.

He cleanses the Temple as if he owns it.

Which is precisely the point this whole week is meant to establish.

Cleansing the Temple

John places this dramatic episode on an earlier visit at the beginning of Jesus' ministry. The Synoptics place it here, which is certainly a more climactic moment and a clearer reason for his antagonists to solidify their resolve to get him out of the way sooner. Of those three, Mark has Jesus enter the Temple briefly, noting the disorder, and returning to Bethany to return next day and clear the place out.

When Matthew and Luke differ from Mark (since each was writing a new edition of Mark) they always have a reason. Here they show the assault immediately on the arrival, which—along with the brouhaha of the triumphal messianic entry—intensifies the tension for the reader better than a delay.

Jesus took *possession* of the Temple! It was the reason he'd come. He will himself become the reconstituted Temple. At his death, the curtain separating the Holy of Holies—the indwelling presence of God—will be slit wide open and flood out into the commonplace world.

Elements to Ponder

Irony

The Pharisees on the hill outside the gate tried to make Jesus rebuke his apostles. They were afraid the Romans would make them responsible if there was an outbreak. But with divine irony, this eruption and the even worse blow-up inside the Temple was precisely what they wanted: a palpable justification for Roman interference. "King of the Jews!"

Exclusivity

To minds so possessed by the idea of God's transcendent selectivity, e.g., qualifications to come close to Yahweh in the Temple, Jesus' defiance of such rules and indiscriminate acceptance of even the most repugnant people—come-one-come-all—was insufferable to his enemies.

It might make us pause ourselves and ponder those excluded from places around our own eucharistic table because of their "unworthiness."

Foal of an Ass

Chesterton describes the Palm Sunday burro:
> With monstrous head and sickening cry
> And ears like errant wings,
> The devil's walking parody
> On all four-footed things.

The paradoxical God rechose the foolish Adam and Eve, barren Abram and Sarai, stammering Moses, spindly David, hill-girl Mary, tempestuous Peter. One of his heroes is a Samaritan renegade, a tax man leaves the Temple justified, the King enters on an ass. King of outsiders, misfits, and public sinners. He eschews the snorting warhorse and conquers in peace.

And a nice touch: He promises it'll be returned.

Peace

What are "the things that make for peace" which Israel had missed? What did its officials fail to appreciate? They valued the Law over human beings, the head over the heart. They were punctilious rather than openhanded; they were the exclusive Chosen, rather than the come-one-come-all of the Kingdom. Again and again—and again—throughout their history prophets had warned them that Hebrew arrogance would be humbled.

Mary, his mother, knew:

> My soul magnifies the Lord, and my spirit rejoices in God my Savior,
>
> for he has regarded the low estate of his handmaiden.
>
> For behold, henceforth all generations will call me blessed;
>
> for he who is mighty has done great things for me, and holy is his name.
>
> And his mercy is on those who fear him from generation to generation.
>
> He has shown strength with his arm, he has scattered the proud in the imagination of their hearts.
>
> He has put down the mighty from their thrones, and exalted those of low degree;
>
> he has filled the hungry with good things, the rich he has sent empty away. (Lk 1:46-53)

It was a way of looking at human life no one had ever seriously considered before.

5. Approaching the Climax

Yom Sheni / Yom Shelishi / Yom Revi'i

(Monday to Wednesday)

No need for prophetic insight. It was inevitable. First, that Jesus couldn't resist going back to the Temple, despite what he'd done there. More likely, because of it. He had taken possession of it, as if it were his. And second, it was equally predictable that those whose most profound beliefs—and livelihoods—he had assaulted would be waiting for him.

As they hiked over the hill of olive trees from Bethany and beheld again the Temple resplendent before them, Jesus suddenly stopped and looked at the enormous gilded building. Then he looked slowly to a small fig tree to his left. He reached up and pawed through the long yellow leaves. There were no figs. Not even the nutty knobs that show the tree will soon bear fruit. But with his hand still clutching the branch, he turned and looked at the Temple turrets golden in the morning sun. "No one," he said, "will eat real figs from you again." One or two tried to tell him it was too early for figs. It would be at least a month. They failed to grasp that he wasn't really talking about the fig tree at all.

After they arrived in the Temple, Jesus and his men strolled in the vast courtyard, his confident voice drawing the curious into their slow eddy of bodies. Some had heard of him; some came every day they could, to enjoy the rabbis' bristly debates. Some merely wanted to assure that their travel expenses were justified. Also, the taste for profit being what it has always been, a few of the hucksters had returned their stalls to their accustomed duly rented places.

Quite likely the group of listeners grew too awkward for walking, so they all found places sitting along the colonnade, with Jesus at their focus. As they listened to ideas of an improbable life in which a loving God expected free cooperation rather than slavish conformity, there was a movement of men at the steps near the lofty central block of sanctuaries.

A delegation of the most elegant and eloquent of the priests strode toward them through the columns of the stoa. They were freshly bathed, secure in certified learning, power, and self-importance. They wore ankle-length white albs, sashed in blue, purple, or scarlet. Even the most junior priests were held "sacred," for no proven virtue or wisdom but because of lineage and learning. Each was allowed his share of meat sacrificed, to use or sell, as well as of Temple contributions after expenses. Most lived lavishly in homes with mosaic floors and muraled walls. The turbans of the priests were conical, the turban of Caiphas, the high priest, was a mushroom puff embroidered in gold. He wore a gold apron of office with a square jeweled chestplate. As high priest, Caiphas presided over the Sanhedrin Council. With puppet King Herod in Galilee, he was chief collaborator keeping the people in line for Rome—the price of keeping their offices. Most priests were hereditary, aristocratic. Most scribes were legalist Pharisees, but no less fastidious.

A scribe had been delegated to speak. "Teacher," he said with a vinegar smile, "we are aware of the . . . of the commotion your arrival occasioned yesterday. As well as the 'incident' with the purveyors licensed by this most holy Temple to provide suitable sacrifices for the faithful. We do desire to be just and reasonable. But our position as guardians of these holy precincts empowers us—in fact, *requires* us— to ask by what *authority* you take it upon yourself to interfere with the essential business of the Temple?"

Jesus murmured to himself. "Business of the Temple." Then he straightened and asked aloud, "Let me clarify first. You men are the arbiters of divine authority, yes? You have been designated by God to authenticate his prophets? Am I correct?"

Most nodded. Cautiously.

"Tell me. Was the baptism and preaching of John authorized by heaven or by humans?"

The spokesman turned to his colleagues with a pinched brow. The official group tightened around itself, whispering. This up-country shyster wasn't going to snare them into their own carefully constructed trap. In this theocracy, *they* were the uncontested, trained, and ordained authority. But he had them immediately pronged on a dilemma. On one side, the ordinary people idolized John. If the priests now denied John was godly, they risked their own credibility. On the other side, if they answered what they really believed—John was unschooled, therefore incapable of true wisdom—they alienated all who believed John had been of God. Worse, if they admitted John spoke for God despite lack of academic credentials, they also yielded that same power to Jesus. This unschooled carpenter from nowhere. And whether they had heard of it or not, John had called Jesus "the Lamb of God," publicly.

The spokesman turned back. "We . . . ," he said, "we are unsure."

Jesus smiled. "Then neither do I need authorization from you."

He spread out his arm, inviting the officials to join the others sitting. But they preferred to stand. "Listen," Jesus said, "tell me what you think of this. Say a man had two sons. The father went to one," and he gestured to those sitting around him, "and he said, 'Son, work in the vineyard today.' But the son stuck out his chin and said, 'No, I won't.' But as the boy walked away, he felt cheap and ungrateful for what he'd said, so he went to work anyway.

Meanwhile, the father went to his other son," and Jesus gestured broadly to the carefully gowned officials, "and he said to him, 'Son, work in the vineyard today,' and the boy bowed and answered, 'Immediately, sir!' But the boy went off with his friends instead. Which boy was a good son?"

The officials grumbled and sniffed, wary of another trap. But a few said, "The first."

Jesus gestured to the people sitting on the steps at his feet. "See? Ordinary people? When John came to you from God, you were skeptical. So were they. But they weren't choked with themselves. Whores and tax collectors went out to him too. And it was their need that responded to John. And they changed their lives. I tell you solemnly: Harlots and highway robbers will walk into the Kingdom of God before you men do."

One or two of them pursed their lips, twitched their skirts, and began to drift toward the sanctuaries. But Caiphas and the others refused to be moved. They stayed, absorbing evidence.

Jesus returned to those sitting along the steps and standing among the pillars, as if the dignitaries had all left. But at times as he went on, he cocked a knowing eye or twitched his head a bit in their direction so only the most dense would miss that he was speaking all along about the aristocrats and priests.

"Another story," he said. "There once was a wealthy farmer who leased his lands out in the country to tenant farmers to work for a fair cut of their yield. So at harvest time, he sent three agents to bring in his share of the profits. But the tenants were fed to the teeth with rents, so they jumped the three, beat one senseless, killed another, stoned the third out onto the road to stumble back to the city. The owner sent another agent whose head they cracked and sent naked back down the highway. The owner was a man of unearthly tolerance so, instead of sending hoodlums to drive out the wicked tenants, as a last resort, he sent his only son. They didn't dare mistreat him. But he was wrong. The tenants were so greedy they said, 'Ah! This is the heir! Kill him, and the land will be ours!' So they dragged him outside the village walls and murdered him. Now just what do you think this unbelievably tolerant landowner ought to do?"

Voices jabbed out from the crowd. "Kill the bastards!" And "Burn 'em out!"

Without looking at the openmouthed officials, Jesus said, "So the Kingdom of God will be taken from those who don't know how to manage it honestly, who mistreat his prophets and hoard what is God's to themselves. It will be given to those who honor their stewardship."

A few young priests bunched their fists and pushed through those at the outer edges of the crowd. But their elders held them back, nodding to the scowling listeners whose eyes were daring them to make another scene. The entourage turned and strode toward the central buildings.

The sun was hot overhead. Some of the onlookers reached furtively into the bags at their belts and tried to slip a bit of flat bread into their mouths. Others less provident looked at them, almost shamefully, at their own lack of foresight. But Jesus merely nodded and, somehow, they grasped his wordless invitation. They pulled from their bags their meager midday meal and, shyly, began sharing it around.

Jesus said, "Allow me another story. Once upon a time there was another wealthy father who arranged a sumptuous banquet for his son's wedding and invited all their friends and relatives. When the date drew near, he sent servants to all the guests reminding them of the feast. But each one hemmed and hawed, pawing around for excuses. 'I, uh, just bought a field and I have to check it out,' and 'Sorry, I just got a team of oxen. I have to break them in.' A third sent word, 'I just got married myself.' The host was enraged. '*Fine!*' he shouted at the servants. 'All of you! Go out to the street corners and around the city gates. Invite the doorway drunks and fancy ladies. Bring in the blind and the cripples and the mangy poor.' The servants came back and said, 'There's still room, sir.' So he said, 'Go out and collar every reprobate you can find. Dump-crawlers and jailbirds! Virtue has nothing to do with it. All they need is to be hungry. The ones I called my friends aren't friends at all!'"

While Jesus had been telling that story, several newcomers drifted from the central buildings to the side of the listeners. Some were priests from the previous onlookers, others were even more richly clothed. A few recognized them as Herodians, ultrarich who supported King Herod and his profitable cooperation with the occupation forces. It was rare to see them coupled with Pharisees who resented the Romans fiercely, if politely. This Jesus had to be a real rogue to make brothers of foxes and jackals.

One courtly Herodian in a scarlet coat edged in gold tracery raised a jeweled finger. "Ah, learned teacher," he said, bowing his head in what could have been read as respect. "We know you have a sterling reputation, unwaveringly true. You are laudably unswayed by baseless popular opinion. Tell us if you will: Is it justified to pay taxes to Caesar?"

The listeners hunched forward. It was beginning to look like a worthwhile debate. This new bunch had him trapped in their own slick dilemma. The census tax could be paid only in the Roman silver denarius. On one side was the Emperor's profile, on the other, the inscription: "Tiberius Caesar Son of the *Divine* Augustus." Good Jews would never even carry such a thing, with a pagan image, except between moneychanger and tax collector. If this new preacher defends taxes, he alienates ordinary people; if he denies them, he's in trouble with the governor.

"Do you have one, a denarius?" Jesus asked. "Let me see it."

To no one's surprise, a Herodian stepped forward with a few coins shining in his palm. One needs pliable principles where money is concerned.

Jesus stepped toward him and nudged the coins. "Whose head is this on the coin? Whose name guarantees its value?"

The Herodian smiled smugly. "Caesar's . . . , sir."

"Simplicity itself," Jesus smiled. "Give Caesar what's his, give God what's his."

They were all flummoxed, even the clever Pharisees. Even the ordinary folk were itching to ask him which was which.

Later that day, or perhaps the next, Jesus was still—or again—talking tirelessly about this whole new way of living he envisioned, where kindness was the truest sign of redemption. As he spoke, various individuals and groups from the Temple sidled near to listen. Few of those sat.

One portly gentlemen edged forward for attention. He was more expensively dressed than many of the other priests, and his many rings bespoke his worth. A Sadducee, the very cream of the priestly aristocracy. To all intents, they *were* the Church/State. He and his fellows busied themselves more with practical matters such as managing the far-reaching Temple enterprises, representing the Hebrew nation to outsiders, acting as religious and civil judges in matters not reserved by the Romans. More hard-nosed than theoretical, and thoroughly conservative. Quite unlike scribes and Pharisees, they dismissed the primeval forest of oral traditions that those others delighted in discussing and fine-tuning, and held only the ancient written Law in any way obligatory. For instance, they denied the resurrection and any afterlife, which were only relatively recent concerns. So the nature of his intervention was quite unexpected.

"Teacher," he said with his impressive voice, "the great Moses enjoined us—or at least that has been claimed by many recent so-called authorities—that, should a man's brother die, leaving his wife childless, the brother must take her for a second wife and do his best to . . . to rectify the situation. But—and I offer this in all seriousness—suppose there were seven brothers. You agree that is quite possible. The eldest died leaving a childless wife, so the next married her. Then *he* died, childless, leaving her to the third. And so on, and so on. Until finally," he pressed his tapered forefinger to his lip to govern a smile, "the long-suffering wife herself—rather widowed-out, you might say—died and entered this afterlife you and others speak of. Which leaves some of us who are less conversant with these otherworld realities in quite a puzzlement. Can you tell us—not merely us priests but these worthy onlookers—in your 'kingdom' whose wife will this woman be? Surely not all seven. Although each of the seven had 'known' her in this life. Can you help us clarify that?"

Jesus himself suppressed a grin. "And one might add, merely for completeness, that the arrangement you mention kept the dead brothers' accumulating property in the family."

"That, too, of course," his inquirer nodded.

Jesus shook his head and chuckled. "You barely know the Scriptures of God, do you? And you surely don't know God. Or what God wants of us."

The Sadducee assumed his full height but held in his anger.

Jesus notched his brow. "You believe in angels, yes?" The Sadducee's mouth pinched. He clearly did not. "They're in the written books, you recall. Abraham's three shining visitors? The two angels who met Lot outside Sodom? Jacob wrestling? An angel passed over Hebrew homes in Egypt daubed with the lamb's blood? God sent Moses the Archangel Gabriel and ninety-nine other angels. You remember that. Yes?"

The other man held a strained silence.

"Since you pose such thorny puzzles," Jesus went on, "let me puzzle you in return. How do you suppose God increases the numbers of his angels? Since, we have to assume, they have no bodies." Jesus continued, but this time to the ordinary people and his Twelve. "You see, there's no need for procreation after the dead have been raised." He chuckled. "Because there's no need for them to be replaced. But that doesn't mean death is the end of *true* life. Remember in the book of Moses, God says to him, 'I am the God of Abraham, Isaac, and Jacob.' Even though all those holy men had left our way of living endless years before Moses. He didn't say 'I *used* to be' or 'I *once* was.' Just as there is no need for birth in heaven, death has no place where God is. With God death *isn't*. God is the God of the living, of the never-dying-again."

Glaring upward, the Sadducee turned and walked back to the Temple. As he passed, a young man—possibly a student scribe—raised a hesitant hand. "Sir," he said, flashing his eyes left and right at his superiors, "what is the greatest of commandments? The root commandment?"

Jesus smiled. "The first thing we say each morning—the *Shema:*
'Hear, Israel, the Lord is our God, the Lord is One.
Blessed be the Name of His glorious kingdom for ever and ever.
And you shall love the Lord your God
with all your heart and with all your soul and with all your might.'"

The young man nodded and smiled.

"But how do we *do* that?" Jesus asked. "That's the only other commandment: we are *kind*. We love God in every other human being as attentively as we love ourselves. That's *all*."

The boy grinned. "Yes, Teacher. That's *all* of it! The rest—all that we study and argue and pick apart. He is one. There is no other. And loving him—with everything we are—and loving our neighbor. You're right. Everything else—*everything* else—is refining perfection!"

Jesus looked at him fondly. "My young friend, you are so close to the kingdom!"

The young man blushed and sat down with the ordinary people.

As they had all day, murmurs dribbled through the crowd. Things like "Have you ever heard a man like this?" and "This man knows. He really *knows*." More than a few muttered "Messiah." Jesus caught the word and turned toward it.

"How would you know if the Messiah had come?" he asked the ordinary listeners. But they were shyly silent. They'd been catechized and faithful but never empowered. Jesus looked over at the Pharisees and priests still listening. "You experts? Whose son will the Messiah be?"

"David's," a few answered.

Jesus chuckled again. "And which of us *can't* claim we're sons of David? And every other king back to Abraham? But don't you find it odd," he said, facing the large group of Pharisees lingering just beyond the common folks. "Isn't it . . . interesting that, when David talks about the Messiah who will come at the great End Time, King David calls The Anointed One 'my *Lord*, my *Master*'? David says that, in his book of Psalms: 'God said to my Master, "Sit here at my right hand until I make your enemies your foot-stool."' You Pharisees know the texts so well. Don't you find that puzzling? I mean, that the great King David would call his distant great-great-great-whatever grandson, 'My *Lord*, my *Master*, my *Superior*'? Can you men help us understand that? You must admit it's strange."

Some of the officials began to drift away; some stayed like moths drawn to flame. But they were quite evidently displeased.

"Watch out for the scribes," Jesus said to the seated people. "They love well-cut, ornate vestments. And long titles. And the best seats wherever they go. They forget there's only one true Master and Lord. And the truly great in *this* life don't need to show it off—the quiet, willing servants. The ones happy to go unnoticed if they can help.

"But God help the Pharisees. Hypocrites! They thicket the path to heaven with laws and undermine it with threats and fear. So joyless they bar others from happiness. Oh, you *worthy* men," he growled. "You prowl land and sea for a single convert, so you can make him as miserable as you are yourselves. Already in hell."

Some of the worthy gentlemen detached themselves and walked back toward the sanctuary, red-faced. Others refused to move. It was worth the obloquy to hear this man write his own death warrant. Some of his own, like Judas, began to be unnerved by this unusual belligerence. Every word he spoke was on fire. But he went on, like a man purging poison.

"Hypocrites! Just to be certain, you give tithes to the Temple of the weeds in your gardens! But what about the *true* Law? How stingy you are with justice and mercy and faith! Blind guides! You strain whatever you drink to avoid a gnat, but you can gag down a camel! You scour the outsides of things and leave the filth inside. Whitewashed bone boxes, gaudy outside, thick with rot inside. You're the sons of those who murdered the prophets, and their skills infest you now.

"A tangle of snakes! And the prophets I'll send to you will get the same—scourging in your synagogues, excommunication, driven from town. On your heads will be the blood of all the new Abels and Zechariahs!"

He stood, silent and exhausted. Then Jesus nodded, first to the elite, then to the ordinary listeners, and he gestured to his own men to follow him out of the Temple.

As they climbed the hill to Bethany, a few noticed that the fig tree they had passed that morning had withered inside and was losing its leaves.

Puzzling Moments

The Fig Tree

Literalists waste a good deal of imagination and ink defending Jesus against cursing an "innocent" fig tree because it had no figs—when no other fig trees did either. The same well-meaning folks feel impelled to defend Jesus' disregard for the pagan owners of the swine near Gadara into which he hurled the "legion" of demons from a madman (MARK 5) and sent them plunging into "the sea." (Even though there is no significant body of water near that town. Surely nothing capable of encompassing "two thousand" swine.) Whether the tree withered or not is hardly the point. Israel had failed in its task of igniting and sustaining the connection between God and the people—which is what "religion" means. But to say that flat out, in a theocracy, would be not only heresy but treason.

This moment is merely a prelude for what will come the rest of this day. Indeed, for the rest of this crucial week.

Authorization

In direct connection to the episode of the fig tree, Jesus has said again and again, "They prove themselves by the fruit they bear. Do you pick grapes from thorn bushes, or figs from thistles?" (MT 7:16). What really empowered those in official Temple robes to think *for* the rest of those in Jesus' audience? They are like the tree, robed in leaves but nothing within.

Despite his lack of formal education, Jesus proves himself enviably skilled at oral examinations. Perhaps those who teach and preach to prepare and sustain Christians in their mission might concentrate less on catechetics (the detailed doctrinal claims of any faith), at which the Temple officials were quite diligent, and more on apologetics (reasons to trust those religious claims). Catechetics requires no more than facile memories; apologetics seeks personal conviction and commitment.

Parables

Each of the three parables resonates the same motif as the fig tree in a different key: Those in charge of religion—i.e., of evoking and sustaining the person-to-person connection of the people with God, those who have undertaken to represent the Master's interests—have failed. They become ensnared in protocol, liturgical and theological niceties, legalism. They have, in effect, taken over the vineyard, the Temple, and turned it into a "business." They have taken the Owner's *place*, which is precisely what Jesus challenged when he assumed control over the Temple yesterday. Their meticulous study and official approbation have gradually blinded them. Their heads have smothered their hearts, which is the only "place" to encounter the living God who was *personally* known to Abraham, Moses, and Jesus.

Of course, Jesus couldn't come right out and say that. Such a naked challenge would be like a Palestinian crying out in a synagogue, a black challenging a Klan rally, hurling a torch into a hayloft. Earlier in the Temple, Jesus had said, "Very truly, I tell you, before Abraham was, I am" (Jn 8:58). And again later, "The Father and I are one" (Jn 10:30). Each time "they picked up stones to throw at him." Once again, he has them at a simmer.

As he so often has, Jesus resorts to parables—stories that, beneath the specifics, tell truths the listeners would reject out of hand if delivered flat-on, literally. The lawyer who asked earlier, "Who qualifies as my neighbor?" would have walked off in a huff if Jesus had answered, "Everybody, especially those you find detestable." So Jesus outfoxed him with the parable of the Good Samaritan. Here, probably with his most innocent look, Jesus asks, "Now just what do you think this unbelievably tolerant landowner ought to do?" The hierarchs have no choice but to answer, "John was of God . . . the first son . . . burn 'em out . . . pay the tax!" Ingenuous as a dove, sly as a serpent. The former, not the latter, quality is overtaught, to the impoverishment of all.

A parable is a parabola, a curve ball. You wrap the truth on an engaging story and whip it past the opposition, who suddenly become aware they've been snookered.

Caesar

Although the strict separation of Church and State has proven an admirably effective way to keep two dragons from one another's fiery throats, no one could legitimately read this as a divine demand for it. Rather, Jesus gives a totally commonsense answer, removing the decision from the hands of both priests and politicians and lodging it exactly where it belongs: squarely on the individual conscience. Which at least suggests that the fundamental task of the churches is not mandating doctrine but teaching individuals to think honestly for themselves: gather evidence, sift out the important, put it into a logical sequence (an outline), draw a conclusion, and ask someone more knowledgeable to critique it. Handier than a pocket catechism.

The struggles of Passion Week keep satellizing around the true meanings of "power."

Hypocrisy

The Sadducee's fakery is transparent. That seventh brother had to be pretty brain-dead obedient to marry that black widow. The case he offers is a rat's nest like those posed to seminarians in moral theology classes: "A Moslem has four wives and wants to convert. . . ." And yet ordinary Christians ask the same kinds of utterly unanswerable questions: "Will my dog be with me in heaven? . . . Will my baldness be cured?" I've done it myself: "If from all eternity God has existed independently of a space and time he hadn't yet created, God must 'dwell' in a realm of reality where those words have no meaning. Then where do they park all those resurrected *bodies*?"

In 1 Corrinthians 15:36, St. Paul gives such speculations about the afterlife their only fitting response: "Those are stupid questions." If the patriarchs are still "alive," they can be alive in some "unearthly" way. Try to exercise your imagination around a "noncorporeal body." And yet, we've all schooled ourselves to say electrons are "impalpable pellets," both ice and steam are water, alcohol is "firewater," bread is flesh, and wine is blood.

The insight not to be lost is that there is *no* sin—not sexual depravity, or divorce and remarriage, or even genocide—against which Jesus inveighs more vehemently or consistently than hypocrisy. And it is impossible to find Jesus flat-out *angry* at any others than the clergy—Temple functionaries and his own ham-headed seminarians.

Elements to Ponder

Authorization

When Claire Booth Luce considered converting to Catholicism, she said she studied Catholics and said in her mind, "You say you have the truth. Well, the truth should set you free, give you joy. Can I *see* your freedom? Can I *feel* your joy?" Those are about the best touch-stone questions I've ever heard for a license to speak about God.

Who do you know who seems to radiate freedom and joy—freedom from the catty remarks of others, joy even when up to the elbows in a hateful job? What would it take a convinced Christian to develop those life-giving attitudes?

Neither diplomas nor ordinations guarantee anything more than the ability to store and recall information, perhaps to engage un-flinchingly in debate, and to speak out confidently. *Jeopardy* skills. Just because a person has supposedly had the Holy Spirit "conferred" on him or her is no guarantee that he or she has had any significant engagement with Her. As to the fig tree's (religion's) "fruits," St. Paul suggests those fruits should be immediately evident in the *person*—not in a stunning ability to quote Scripture chapter-and-verse, or canon law, or *The Catechism of the Catholic Church.* Nor can the evidence of the presence of God's Spirit within anyone be tested by any multitude of questions or lab tests. For Paul, it can only be "sensed" from the unreflective habits the individual reveals in every-day life: "love, exuberance, serenity, patience, kindness, generosity, fidelity to commitments, tolerance and self-possession" (GAL 5:22).

Don't just read the list. Take each one by itself. Think of an individual who easily manifests that one. Is it possible you know anyone who demonstrates *all* of them?

Heart

The first sign of a dying society is a new edition of the rules. It's a tacit admission that the enterprise can no longer count on the

Spirit to keep it alive and moving and growing. Some rabbis numbered 613 separate commandments in the Law, of which 248 were positive demands and 365 were prohibitions. Some were "light," some "heavy" (e.g., "venial" and "mortal"). A great deal of rabbis' time together was spent debating "weights." The 1983 Code of Canon Law has 1,752 canons. Jesus has only two, neither of which admits of any loopholes.

Academic Learning

Some who have not read him carefully misquote Thomas a Kempis as being a hardened anti-intellectual who said any time spent with a book was wasted and that it was better to have compunction than to know how to define it. This is yet one more example of the lethal dualism that has infected humans from the start, the reassuring certainty that comes from reductionism: hard-edged either/or's rather than more fluid more-or-lesses. Students fed up with courses that seem utterly impractical say, "You can get a *lot* more learning on the street and from personal experience without having your nose in some *book* all the time." As if it had to be one or the other. Because of their inexperience with reflective thinking and wider perspectives, their reduction neglects to factor in the truth that the books' authors—and even their most sheltered teachers—have had more experience than they have, not to mention the skill to distill those experiences into words. What's more, only a naive fool feels the need to reinvent the wheel.

Sneering at those privileged to be well read is of course often justified. Some people write learned theses on love but won't greet anyone in the corridor. But it would be not merely unjust but stupid to misread Jesus as antilearning. The Gospels are often mystifying to modern readers simply because Jesus presumes a thorough acquaintance with the only books available to a Jew of his time.

Any virtue, unbalanced by its polar opposite, runs amok into a vice. Humility without confidence becomes stagnation, chastity without passion becomes sterility. The generous enthusiasm of liberals must be balanced by the prudence of conservatives—and the timidity of the cautious needs the ignition of the bold. Just so, God endowed humans with intelligence so that we can figure things out, so that we needn't yield dumbly to weather and disease and unruly nature, but we have the wits to figure things out. Nor does each generation have to start from scratch. That's what libraries—and Google—are for. In the same way, the fragile architecture of intellectual theory needs always to be grounded deep in the earthy. That is what the incarnation is all about. As Pope Francis said: "The shepherd should smell of sheep."

"Uncontested, Trained, and Ordained Authority"

Any attempts to argue that the Church is a democracy are ill-advised. Not to mention frustrating and doomed. Yet to treat the Church solely as a monarchy—dualism, reductionism—is impoverishing as well as insulting to laypeople whose academic credentials are often far-and-away beyond their pastor's and even their bishop's.

Although all the power is—and perhaps even must be—on one side, all the worthwhile ideas to enrich "Church" and "our religion" are not restricted to the ecclesiastically trained and ordained. As witness all the voices of the Hebrew Scriptures whom we hold holy and God-sent, not to mention the first witness to the resurrection: a laywoman out of whom Jesus had driven seven devils (Mk 16:9). Buddha, Aristotle, Mary of Nazareth, Joan of Arc, Francis of Assisi, Teresa of Avila, Catherine of Siena, Thomas More, Nicholas Owen, Rene Goupil, Bernadette Soubirous, Dorothy Day, Tillich, Reinhold Niehbuhr, Mother Teresa. None of them ordained clerics. Therese of Lisieux had the rough equivalent of grammar school and was a wretched speller, but she is a Doctor of the Church.

Some crucial elements of what being Catholic means are more tellingly clear to troops in the trenches than to the academically trained officers at HQ, and ignoring them imperils even the validity and effectiveness of HQ decisions. Hebrew Job could look at Yahweh and have every right to ask, "Do you have any idea how this *feels*?" But if Job were to look up to the crucified Son and ask that question, God could answer truly, "Yes. Now I do."

The incarnation assured us God was literally down-to-earth. His representatives owe it to him to be the same.

6. Impending Storms

Early in the Week

After the long and wearying day on his feet, Jesus stopped the Twelve as they labored up the side of the Mount of Olives, and they sat shielded under the trees from the westering sun. One of them said, "Teacher, look! How splendid the Temple is in the sunset! Those huge stones, like giants holding one another up! It would take an earthquake . . ."

Jesus blew air from his lungs and shook his head sadly. "All for nothing," he sighed. "I tell you truly, not one stone will be left atop another. It will all come crashing down."

They all tensed. Judas seemed more disconcerted than the rest.

Simon Peter spoke hesitantly for them all. "When?" he asked. "We were hoping . . ."

"When I'm gone," Jesus said, and some winced, "be wary of false prophets who tell you I sent them. Their way will be easier. Smoother. But diabolically clever, tempting. Just look at that great city! All that gilded glory. Everything you've valued for a lifetime!" He threw out his hand to the magnificent golden edifice across the valley, "It will all come tumbling down with greater thunder than when Joshua blew his horns outside Jericho. But nothing compared to what will finally come one day. Just a blurry image of the very end.

"Oh, in the meantime you *will* suffer for my sake. I've warned you before, but you stayed. Our fellow Jews will drag you into the synagogues. You'll be beaten up. Worse. The Gentiles will come for you, too, because your lives will confound them. Be confident when they hand you over, as they'll hand me over. I'm here to show you *how*. Your own brothers will give you over as heretics. Your fathers will treat you as dead. Even your own children will betray you because of me. But you're *not* alone. *Never alone.* My Spirit is now rooted deep inside you. Forever and ever. You'll learn to understand that, too. Be resolute and faithful, and you'll never be truly lost. I promise!

"Just don't lose your heads. This is only the journey *toward* the end. And that End of Everything won't come till my good news has reached the very ends of the earth.

"You're wondering *when* will the Temple fall? Remember in Daniel? When invaders set up the sacrilegious image in the inner Temple, and God's wrath descended on the city? It will happen again. When that does happen, then you should move. If you're in the city, gather your families and make for the hills, even in winter, even on the Sabbath. If you're out in the fields, don't be a fool and stop to pack. God help pregnant women. But God will not let that catastrophe last forever.

"Watch out for the doomsday mongers. There are always wars and rumors of wars. Famines, earthquakes. That's just the way the world works. Keep levelheaded. Remember, there'll be signs that *seem* like the very final signs. The doomsayers will come out from under every rock. 'Oh, woe!' they'll say, 'But we've found the Messiah! He's over the Mount of Olives in the wilderness. He's right inside here! For a few shekels I can introduce you.'

"Oh, my friends, when the Son of Man finally does come, you'll know it, all right! It will be clear as a sheet of lightning from one end of the sky to the other. The sun and moon and stars will come streaking out of the heavens. The whole earth will tremble like palsy.

"Remember Daniel again. How the Great Ancient of Days took his blazing throne in the heavens, his robes and hair white as hoarfrost, tens upon tens of thousands in attendance on him. Then striding across the heavens comes a Son of Man! They lead him to the Ancient One, who lays on his strong shoulders dominion, and glory, and a kingdom. So that all people, all nations, all languages, should serve him. A kingdom of forever. Which can never be destroyed.

"With a call of trumpets, the Son of Man will send out his angels to the four winds to bring his beloved ones home, good and bad, alive and dead. That's the sure sign the end has come.

"When? What I said of the Temple? Some of you will actually witness it. So be vigilant. But of the final coming of the Son of Man, no one knows. Not the angels of heaven. Not even the Son. Only the Father. So live your lives always alert, awake to the length and breadth and depth of the hidden world you now know you dwell in. Don't let your hearts be dragged down, dulled by drunkenness or dribbled away on trivial daily distresses. Pray you never live shallow lives. So that, no matter when the End is, you can at any time in your life stand without fear before the Son of Man.

"Try to understand this by remembering a time this happened before, the time of Noah. Everybody was going about their daily business—eating, drinking, marrying, getting dinner ready. *No* warning. Then *crash*! Two working side by side in a field. One's taken away, one's left behind. Two women grinding meal, two asleep in one bed. One's taken, one's left.

"Think about the stories I've told, too, about the worthy and the unworthy. So many times. Remind yourselves of the two servants, the one the master comes home and finds wasting his goods with ne'er-do-wells, the other handing him a house even better than when the master went away. And the others, too. Like the bridesmaids, when the groom was late calling for his new bride, some empty-handed and others with lamps lit, ready to serve them. No matter when. And the story of the talents—how two servants took a risk and doubled what the master had left them, but the other poor timid failure. Too self-doubting to take a chance. Remember, he'd done nothing *wrong*. He just had no faith in what the master had entrusted him with."

As usual, Simon Peter voiced what most of them were wondering. "And what will it be like, then? When this Son of Man comes. What will he expect of us? What should we be vigilant *about*? What will please God?"

Jesus nodded. "When the Son of Man comes, surrounded by the angels who've gathered all the people, he'll sit on his throne of glory. And he'll divide the ones who lived rightly from the ones who missed the whole point. The same way every evening a shepherd separates sheep on his right from goats on his left.

"To the sheep on his right, he'll say, 'Welcome! So welcome! Into the kingdom of joy you've been preparing yourselves for. It's been waiting for you since the creation of the world! You're the ones who truly loved God. When I was hungry, you fed me. Thirsty and you shared your cup, friendless and you sheltered me, naked and you covered me, sick and you cared for me. I'm so grateful to you. Come!

"But the sheep will stand befuddled. And they'll say, 'But, uh, when did we see you . . .?'

"'Whenever you saw anyone in need and reached out in kindness, it was me.'

"And off they'll go, singing and thumping one another's backs, to the endless Banquet.

"Then the Son of Man will turn sadly to those left behind. 'And you. I still love you. But you never found out what love really means, how gifted you were. So you never felt grateful. I was hungry, thirsty, lost, naked, imprisoned, sick. I was mocked, belittled, excommunicated. You chose not to notice. Blocked me out. You thought love meant something else. You chose to live as if I weren't there. Which is where you'll continue to be. Where I am not.' And those dismissed, absolutely incapable of complaining that the judgment is unjust, will go away, lost in eternal lovelessness."

And they sat there for a very long time in silence.

No one knows exactly when, but sometime when it was least likely to be noticed, Judas slipped away from the group. As keeper of the common purse, he was always running errands, looking for provisions, begging shelter for the night, dispensing alms. Judas had a fine-honed sense of the outsider, the misused, the luckless. Had the others been more attentive to his unspoken clues, they would have sensed his unease. It might have been that, converted unswervingly to the Kingdom Jesus offered, he now believed that true power lay in serving the weak and needful and in no way vested in earthly power or pomp or punishment.

He could have been reading these last days in a different light from the less clever disciples. The wild reception on their arrival at the city gates, the shouts about Jesus the new David, the *earthly* king—which Jesus made no move to refute or refuse. Then Jesus' stunning ferocity and overt physical demonstration in the Temple. Beyond that, the unaccustomed belligerence of his daylong debates challenging the lawyers, the guardians of the Temple, and the royalists. Now this revolutionary warlike talk even of destroying the magnificent Temple?

All the events of this weekend were so distant from these three years of caring hand-to-hand for the poor, the leprous, the misfits, the twisted and misunderstood. The people Jesus loved despite themselves. Just as Judas himself did.

No matter Judas's motive; the testimony is clear that he found a way to speak to High Priest Caiphas in private, and through him to the Temple police.

"What will you give me," he reportedly asked, "if I show you a way to take him without creating a disturbance in the city? I know you want him. I can show you a way."

The religious leaders were more than gratified for such an unexpected blessing. A true son of Abraham and a patriot, trying to protect his faith and his nation from the reprisals of the infidels. They offered him thirty pieces of silver. And he took it.

From that moment on, it was merely a matter of time.

Puzzling Questions

Prediction

The earliest extant Christian document is 1 Thessalonians (51 CE, only seventeen years after the Passion events). It uses some of the same words of Jesus ("according to the Lord's own word," [4:15]): clouds, gathering the elect, angels, lawlessness, apostasy, defilement of God's temple, the *parousia* (final arrival of the Son of Man) coming as a thief, sudden destruction of the wicked, and so on. Therefore, that letter of Paul came *before* the historical destruction of Jerusalem in 70 CE and thus suggests not only that the community was convinced Jesus had actually foreseen it but that they held a belief in an *imminent* End of Everything.

Prediction isn't all as arcane as we might envision it—witches staring into their cauldrons and watching liquid videotapes of future events. Every parent engages in it continuously: "You better watch yourself, young man!" No crystal ball involved. They've been around the track more often and, every time they've seen such-and-such actions, they inevitably resulted in the same unhappy effects. The entire Hebrew Scripture records God's *consistent* response to Israel's misreading of the whole point of their relationship/covenant.

This long speech (probably a conflation of many), despite minor differences in each version, makes the same points in all: (1) the two events—destruction of the Temple and the End—are two *separate* events, the first being a kind of foretaste of the latter but not itself one of the signals that the other is immediately forthcoming; (2) Jesus is a prophet of The Plan; (3) the Jewish nation's fate is linked to its reaction to Jesus; (4) Each version of the speech is one more instruction preparing the inner Twelve to undergo adversity; (5) Each encourages steadfast resilience because God will not be overcome. Like each segment of this book, the speech is a combination of stories, explanations, and exhortations gathered into a single summary.

In the Synoptics, this serves as a kind of farewell address to the inner group, similar to but less spiritual than John's very long address at the Last Supper. This is like a teacher reviewing before the final, harrowing examination. It works the themes of purging and triumph. But it should not give "aid and comfort" to those who confuse the Son of Man with the economy-generated Santa Claus who's "making a list, checking twice," constantly spying, so he can swoop down on those who have been naughty and not nice. In the context of all Jesus said about laws and the heart, this final homily doesn't call for ever-watchful scrupulosity. Jesus' unfailing generosity with sinners through his entire public life negates any possible such misreading.

Apocalyptic

"Apocalyptic" is a word we're remotely familiar with from numerous "after the end" films. *War of the Worlds* has been a perennial since H. G. Wells published it in 1898. But the stimulus for "What will it be like?" stories has been around for as long as humans have had imagination and wonder. "How will all this end?" (Since just about everything humans most value usually does come to an end.) Which triggers yet another question: "Meanwhile, what is everything *for*? When the Creator steps back in and asks for a tally, what will the Creator expect that we've done?" The question is the same as Aristotle's search for the "final cause" of everything—"final" as in *finis*: "aim, purpose." What can we discover in the programming of anything that reveals its proper use? Which leads to yet another profound question: "Is there, in fact, a Programmer?"

But the strict definition of "apocalyptic"—too easily used as a synonym for "The Atomic Simplification"—is rightly limited to *scriptural* attempts to deal with "eschatology." That means not just The Four Last Things: Death, Judgment, Hell, and Glory, but also the effect those realities have in forming the objective background against which we can judge our true success as creatures of

God in the present life. Within that matrix/web/framework we judge the long-range purpose and value of everything that exists within it. Atheists simply deny that such a matrix, what I've called "The Really Real," exists. In fact, they deny it *can* exist, since it is nonmaterial. If they are right, then there simply is no objective value to anything, except for whatever spurious "value" each of us subjectively chooses to assign, for as long as we manage to last.

Further, "apocalyptic" is a peculiar (pun intended) approach to eschatology—the "End" of Everything, in both the sense of ultimate destiny and proximate purpose. The Greek root of "apocalyptic" means "unveiling," and one is tempted to explain it crudely by comparing it to slow "strip tease." Recall the old show-biz motto: "It's better to conceal than reveal." It is "underground" writing, a code based on allusions and symbols known only to those "in on it." You find it in the OT books of Zechariah, Joel, especially in Ezekiel and Daniel, and in the NT in profusion in the mystifying book of Revelation. Some of the symbols are bizarre, e.g., multiheaded dragons, enormous crashing statues. But many are multicultural: a valley of bones, crowns, eyes, fire, planets. In a remarkably mild manner, the evangelists use it in this final sermon.

Most Christians who are otherwise well educated nonetheless find the symbols of "apocalyptic" writing baffling. No problem. The experts are baffled, too, just more rightfully confident. I personally have never been comfortable with apocalyptic. It reminds me of fever dreams—or what, I'm told, erupts in the drug-baffled psyche. Like all symbol-drenched writing it invites—almost begs for—equally bizarre responses and grave robbing for "significance." Without a disciplined, educated grasp of how *first-century* Jewish and Greek minds resonated to these symbols—what the writers presumed they'd grasp—the result can be more anarchic than the original bewildering documents seem to the modern reader. And the very best of the professional scholars at times seem as if they're trying to force Jackson Pollock to defend every single drip.

The discourse predicts both the destruction of Jerusalem (which had happened *before* all but Paul and Mark were written) and the end of the whole world. In the apocalyptic style, it's vexingly difficult to disentangle which "end" is being discussed at any given verse. To the Hebrew mind (and the Eastern mind in general), the transcendent dimension of reality—the Really Real—is intimately *interwoven* with the events of the everyday world. In what they write, it requires educated hunches to separate "right now" from "inside the Big Picture." (Recall the distinction between "historical" and "meaningful." The time-machine photographer would not have recorded a great feathered angel in Our Lady's kitchen. If Peter, James, and John had actually beheld—with their physical eyes—Jesus transfigured with Moses and Elijah, how could they have remained so implausibly dense?)

At its most primitive, in this hyperenriched perception of human life, the gods are actually *within* objects of this world like thunder and sunsets. Yahweh described himself to Moses as "I am who am": the pool of existence out of which everything draws its "is." Hopkins wrote, "The world is *charged* with the grandeur of God." Even hard-nosed scientists now declare that the rock that skinned my knee is not solid at all but aswarm with whirring particles—and most of it is empty space. Therefore, it would be easy, even inevitable, for writers to conjoin the actual fall of Jerusalem with the End of Everything, since all the Temple meant had been the core of their "reality." It did, historically, end the Temple as a focus for international Judaism. Forever.

Desecrating Abomination / "The Sacrilegious Image"

This is an allusion—for those "in on" the Hebrew books—to an event in 167 BCE. Antiochus IV, the Seleucid Emperor, trying to cow the stubborn Hebrews, erected a pagan statue of Zeus Olympius in the Temple. In describing it (and the promise of Yahweh's vengeance for the abomination), the book of Daniel skirted reprisals by writing as if it were a *history* of a pagan desecration years earlier (606 BCE)—much as the French Resistance openly staged plays mocking Adolf Hitler under the guise of a historical work about the mad emperor Caligula.

So here, an allusion back to Daniel, for those who knew it, covers a dangerous assertion about the Emperor Caligula (ruled 37–41 CE), who wanted a statue of his divine self erected there but died before the order could be executed. Then his successor, Nero (54–68), already a butcher of Christians, planned the same thing. ("Whoever reads this will understand" [Mk 13:14]). The Jewish reaction to those attempts, as well as evidence of malfeasance by Roman appointees, ignited the Jewish War. Both of these attempts were after Jesus.

Whereas Jesus almost surely did warn of the literal downfall of Judaism, little problem that the three Gospel writers (other than Mark) who wrote *after* the cataclysm of 70 *superimposed* specific details onto Mark's original rough sketch, from what they later saw in the prophecy's fulfillment.

Had the writers been given to fabrication in order to convince their listeners Jesus was a "genuine" prophet, they could have made his foretelling even more specifically astute. Since the events he "supposedly" predicted had already historically occurred, they might have locked in their case for Jesus' detailed foresight by making his predictions even less easily avoidable—and probative: "In thirty-seven years a future emperor (whose name will start with "T") will surround the city, with three legions called Five, Twelve, and Fifteen (V Macedonica, XII Fulminata, XV Apollinaris) on the western side and a fourth called Ten (X Fretensis) where olives grow in the east. They will breach its walls, killing a million, leading one hundred thousand into slavery."

That would be catnip for modern doomsayers and astrologers, like "when a black Shintoist will be named First Mother of the largest Christian family." They resisted the temptation.

Just Jerusalem or Everything?

Surely if Jesus' foretelling the fall of the Temple were a signal for the final, historical, inescapable End in the *proximate* future, all warnings to get out Jerusalem would be useless—unless one had access to a spaceship (Cf. Miller, *A Canticle for Leibowitz.*) Getting out of one city could hardly outdistance the faithful from the end of the whole world.

That insight might help separate the two shuffled-together predictions: In sections that suggest immediate actions, the writers picture Jesus offering hints about the immediate future, e.g., the desecrating image in the Temple. Whenever he offers advice for long-range expectations, he's motivating exemplary living in a reality certainly curtailed by one's own literal death, but without any pointed reference to a literal End of Everything.

When death arrives, there'll be no U-Hauls at the back of our hearses. For those of us two thousand years later, it suggests that we who are comfortable ought to have a broader perspective on the true value of our possessions in this (very) long background that transcends death.

What's more, the experienced reader ought always to remember, first, that the Kingdom Jesus is predicting is not a *worldly* kingdom, where buildings collapse to make way for a new ruler, but a union of souls with the divine Spirit, who is the living love of the Father and Son. Also keep in mind that the original audiences for these four books, unlike ourselves today, were actually, literally facing just such betrayals and brutality. It was that long haul Jesus was also warning them about. What Jesus suggests is advice for *any* time of severe distress: calm faith, since a trustworthy Father is in ultimate control. To bypass that wisdom for the titillation of apocalyptic scares is just plain horror-movie silly. A roller-coaster ride trying to shed light on what is actually, for most of us, a marathon where winning is less important than tenacity.

However, like tarot cards and séances, it's great fun—no matter how unfounded—to read cosmic significance into what is, objectively, simply the ways human living-together tends to work, given that every one of the participants except One is imperfect, and clumsy, and selfish.

Judging with the experience of the last two thousand years, we cannot think Jesus meant the literal immediate end of the world. The alternative would be that he was a lunatic or a liar. What's more, it would be the height of arrogance to say he then must have meant the generation you and I happen to inhabit.

Another distinction Jesus makes is that the *time* of the second coming is *unknown*, even to the *Christ*! Therefore, destruction of the Temple is predicted in the *proximate* future ("Some standing here who will not taste death before they see the kingdom of God" [LK 9:27]). Most important: The final prerequisite for the second coming is the evangelization of all nations (MT 24:14). Literalists should calm their fear until the newscaster reports that the moon is now on a beeline course for Kokomo, Indiana, and "Stars Fell on Alabama Last Night." And when you feel a tingle in your skull like when Captain Kirk said, "Beam us up, Scotty!" No need to pack or run. (But first check that the reporter isn't H. G. Wells or Orson Welles.)

The Temple's end is a brief prefiguring of the real thing—at a *purposely* unspecified date. All theology is sufficient evidence that God invites exploration but defies conquest.

Further, anyone who has read the Gospels thus far has no reason to be scandalized if the original disciples seem to have gotten something mixed up.

The Literal End of Jerusalem

In 66 CE, Nero sent an army under Vespasian to quell a Jewish uprising. By 68, most resistance outside the capital had fallen, but Nero killed himself, and Vespasian was named emperor. His son Titus got the task of eliminating all Hebrew opposition. By

70, the Romans had breached the outer walls, setting everything on fire, gutting the Temple of its gold and relics for museums in Rome. To all intents and purposes, Judaism no longer had a true central focus.

An Imminent End of This World

It seems unavoidable that at least a goodly number of early Christians expected the literal End to come in their lives. "Will not taste death." was too readily applied not just to being alive for the end of the Temple but for the End of Everything. There have always been people who consider the mess the world is in and itch to be the first one to say, "Look! Up in the sky! It's a bird! It's a plane! It's . . . the Son of Man!" No doubt Jesus did describe it as "at any moment." He could have meant "any moment *now*" or just as likely "any moment when you least expect it." Speculation yields to humility. And Jesus said even *he* didn't know the time.

Since that moment hasn't come in two thousand years, the only legitimate connection between the two ends is that the destruction of 70 was, truly, the end of Judaism's unifying heart, the end of "their whole world" as it had given background-value to their lives. In its place came a brand-new life focus: a Son of Man coming from his tomb into his kingdom, which is "*not* of this world." The World End triumph is unspecified, but the *kairos*—the crucial moment in time—is just around the corner as Jesus is speaking to them. And in the coming week Jesus will face that *kairos* in utter loneliness.

This final exhortation has also given rise to a dualism still evident in many prayers of the Catholic liturgy in which words are put into the community's mouths declaring that we hope to deny the values of "this world" and focus our eyes solely on the *true* values of "the next world." If we are supposed to be saying that whatever we hold precious in this life is mere trash, that attitude is rankly unchristian. It surely is an unwitting insult to the Creator of everything in this world. Not to mention an implicit denial of a core Christian doctrine: the incarnation, in which God himself willingly and thoroughly enmeshed himself in all things human. Genuine Christians do not disdain this world but instead try to "find God in all things." Our present world is rooted in The Really Real and constantly giving us flashes of it.

Along that same line: Unlike fairly recent apocalyptists like Jim Jones and David Koresh, real Christians don't run to suicide to escape into a better life. On the contrary, original Christians did everything in their power and imagination to continue to be Christians and avoid death.

One Taken, One Left

Many miss the diametric contrast between the hyperdramatic apocalyptic warning signs and the bland description of the End in both Matthew and Luke which compares it to "the days of Noah." How did Yahweh end it all the *last* time?

"One taken, one left behind." Which is which? Taken away to damnation or to salvation? Left behind with the Son of Man or with his Enemy? Or even left behind to start the whole thing over again, as it was in the time of the Flood? As above, such open-ended symbols and statements are catnip to the imagination—and then to courageously ignorant assertions.

But the reference to Noah puts some limit on what Jesus intended. That allusion at least suggests that the righteous are carried away safe and the wicked are abandoned, as in the Flood. Matthew's Last Judgment says the same with sheep and goats. And the Flood came *without* warnings. People were simply going about business as usual— eating, drinking, marrying, preparing dinner. Two in one bed or at the grain mill. One saved, the other abandoned? That question is also answered in the story of the Last Judgment: The key is their ingrained attitude and response to the hungry, thirsty, naked, and needy. Their consistent habit of *kindness*.

The Afterlife

"Metempsychosis," the transfer of the soul from one state or host to another, has been a staple of stories nearly forever. It evidences a radical belief in the incorruptibility of the human soul/self, especially in the reincarnation espoused by Eastern religions. Prehistorical societies buried their dead with provisions for a continued journey. Although Hebrew concern for another life was late arising (Sadducees ignored it), the resurrection of Jesus, defeating the possibility of annihilation by death, is the core Christian doctrine. First Thessalonians, the very first extant Christian writing, says: "Then we who are alive, who are left, will be caught up in the clouds together with them to meet the Lord in the air; and so we will be with the Lord forever" (4:17).

John Donne and Edgar Allen Poe were fascinated by the idea. In Joyce's Ulysses, Molly Bloom calls it "Met him pike hoses"; David Foster Wallace has a character named Madame Psychosis in *Infinite Jest*. More recently, The Rapture has had its fifteen spotlight minutes. Adherents believe that, prior to the time of the Great Tribulation, God will supernaturally "whisk away" all Christians into heaven, while the unprepared return for another bout with the Tribulation. Even *Family Guy* and *The Simpsons* have climbed aboard the Rapture. (Easier than Scripture.)

Somewhere in that thicket of symbols, I wonder if there might be room to wedge in the idea of purgatory, for which there is almost no scriptural evidence. For whatever reasons, the official Church has disenfranchised limbo. Small loss. But some otherwise knowledgeable folks think purgatory was also demolished. And (many hope) hell as well.

There is little scriptural concern for eternal punishment and almost no evidence for a belief in some transitory punishment (purgatory). But certainly, even those who have never cracked *The Divine Comedy*—and all cartoonists and moviemakers—owe more of their beliefs about the afterlife to Dante than to the Scriptures.

(Note: I'm assuming Dante was not an eyewitness reporter come back.)

Personally, I can't imagine how a reasonable God could *not* have a hell and a purgatory. Not two "places" (not in an afterlife where time and space have no meaning anymore). But—in fairness to the individual's free choices—there *has* to be a "dimension" for those who simply do not *want* to be where God is, where there's need to submit one's intelligence and freedom to Anyone else. And, in fairness, there at least ought to be a "dimension" for those who are not yet capable of joy. Puritans, the humorless, the faultfinding, the scrupulous—all those who in this life believed they were either far more or far less important than they really are.

I offer that alternative with no more basis than the Church has used for centuries, the fact of its congeniality, its "fitness."

And just as hell needn't be an endlessly fascinating series of Dantean sadisms, neither need purgatory be a place of humiliation where the proud have their heads bent by rocks on their necks. Why not long sessions with an insightful psychotherapist (soul-doctor) to discover, slowly and yet truly painfully, where one has missed the point again and again?

As with the pairs in the Noah reference—eating, drinking, marrying, getting dinner ready—the only problem with those "left behind" was not seeing their ordinary lives in the perspective of the transcendent, the Really Real.

Judas

Throughout, I have been editorializing about Judas, just as the evangelists did. John, out-and-out, offering no other evidence, calls him "a thief." Luke says, "Satan had entered into him." But what kind of understanding would an actor need in order to get inside his skin—honestly? To find Judas's "subtext"? Every human, the central figure of his or her story, has to feel "justified." Even Hitler never did anything inhuman apart from a law exonerating it. As Dorothy Sayers wrote: "One thing is certain: [Judas] can't have been the creeping, crawling, patently worthless villain that some simple-minded people would like to make out; that would be to cast too grave a slur upon the brains or character of Jesus."

Each of us has to confess a strong bias against Judas from our earliest Bible stories and endless sermons thereafter. And yet, whoever Judas was, and whatever he did at the end, he had *not* deserted, as many others did when Jesus said his followers had to eat his flesh and drink his blood (JOHN 6). Judas *did* stay. He could have resigned. He could have given up his vocation as the rich young man had. But he stayed. No one I've ever read seems to have asked why.

Whenever he's mentioned, even long before his treachery, he's described as the traitor. Like a family's black sheep who's brought disgrace on them all. They'd spent three years with him, companions, sharing blistering days and icy nights. Quite likely he had little imagination, little tolerance for ambiguity, but he also likely was best at things the town rabbi expected from docile classes. Probably not the easiest man to like because he acted so sure of himself, but they'd loved him as they loved the other spiky men in the community, and they felt free to share their fears and confusions. He was shrewd and knew the value of things, their quartermaster: he kept them fed and found them lodging; he was the one the poor knew they could go to. For some reason, Jesus entrusted the purse to Judas, not to Matthew who had been a professional.

In the episode of Mary and the spikenard, when Jesus upbraided him in front of everybody, he was "only doing his job," showing genuine concern over needless waste. He was trying to watch the purse and provide for men who'd clearly stopped providing for themselves. And yet, in front of everybody, he was put down. No one seems to suggest Judas was jealous of Jesus' three pets—Peter, James, and John—although the evidence suggests he was more acute than any of them, and the way he ended his life suggests he was a deep brooder.

Unlike the fishermen and Matthew, we have no clue to his calling. But Sayers offers the intriguing possibility that Judas had been a terrorist. His conversion like Che Guevara's turning from armed revolt to working nonviolently for the disenfranchised.

And Judas was *really* converted, she suggests. He wasn't like the Zebedees who bowed their heads at everything Jesus said but still craved that old power. In a very real sense, Judas was the first "born-again Christian." Like all uncomplicated, generous, very recent converts, he was the True Believer—110 percent.

But all the events of this weekend—the imperial ride and the shouting, the imperious attack on the moneychangers, the masterful crushing of the opposition's objections, and finally the uncompromising prediction that the Temple itself would come crashing down. It was too much, Sayers suggests. Judas believed Jesus was duped by power. He had sold out the dream!

So, out of *love*, Judas betrayed Jesus to save him from himself.

Pure speculation. But no more groundless than accusing him of being a thief all along.

Elements to Ponder

Fear as a Motive

Fear is the absolutely basest motive for moral integrity. Like hope of reward—a treat, a cookie, heaven—it's effective with subhumans and to the animal responses we share with them. It has proven ever so effective since the outset of Christianity—excommunication, *auto da fe*, *The Syllabus of Errors*. Effective, but not always laudable. Or Christlike. Mature Christians no longer seek integrity to avoid hell or to gain heaven but to please Someone they know and love.

Someone in search of a doctoral thesis topic in theology might consider the psychological fusion in the American imagination—from earliest childhood—of the Advent of Jesus blending with the even-more-insistent "Santa Claus Is Comin' to Town." I suggest it not just facetiously. As Pavlov's dog merged the bell sound and salivating, children, long before they're capable of critical discernment, hear that both Jesus and Santa are on their way. Which one "sees you when you're sleeping, knows when you're awake"? Doesn't Mom say God is always watching (over) me? Which one is "makin' a list, checkin' it twice, gonna find out who's naughty and nice"? Is that like what we're supposed to do preparing for reconciliation?

To repeat: not just trivial speculation.

In the moral practice of Jesus throughout the Gospels, no sinner is ever asked a list of specific sins or their number, no one is ever given a penance. Those who, in order to help the young understand human frailty and the need for readjustment, resort to the economic metaphor of debt and reimbursement, betray a radical misunderstanding of *all* Christianity means.

Perspective

One major purpose of these pages is to draw attention to the *most* necessary attitude to comprehend this Holy Week: a willingness to accept confidently that the very smartest atheists are wrong. Protagoras asserted, "Man is the measure of all things." Wrong. Carl Sagan's opening sentence in Cosmos—"The cosmos is all there is and all there ever was and all there ever will be" is unjustified. To comprehend Christianity, or any other religion, in any more than a surface, sheerly rational sense, one has to be at the very least open to the *possibility* that Reality is not limited by the human "equipment" we have to access and analyze and evaluate it fairly.

It requires before all else that one accepts that anything *can* be "holy."

Fifty years of teaching apologetics to the young has made me believe that such a susceptibility is no longer an attitude we can presume. Just as the stars have now been washed out of our awareness by a profusion of artificial lights, so our demand for concrete certitude and iron-clad guarantees has neutered our ability to sense the "holy," what Bonhoeffer called "The Beyond in Our Midst." One is tempted to believe that, even for most practicing adult believers, the force of the transcendent has been blunted, then withered into Hallmark lip service.

But if such brilliant and articulate critics as Protagoras, Sagan, Christopher Hitchens, and Richard Dawkins are correct and this life is "all there is," then the only framework within which we can pass any judgment on our own personal value/meaning/purpose are the four parameters of time and space. However, against a timeline that extends for nearly fourteen billion years, my eighty-or-so years are as trivial as a burp in hurricane. If, like Hitler, I could conquer all Europe, half of Russia, and the whole of North Africa, in the objective universe that stretches incomprehensibly outward, all that land doesn't even show. If I grasp some sense of validation and self-worth from my "accomplishments"—my ten exemplary children, my two Nobel prizes, my shelf of publications—what weight do they carry against the objective background of the present population of China, the perspective of human history—from the first control of fire to splitting the atom, to the expanse of shelves in the whole Library of Congress?

Given limits imposed on what *can* be "reality" by Protagoras, Sagan, Hitchens, and Dawkins, even those judgments are unfounded and vacuous, since "purpose" is a nearly universal delusion.

Many in Lilliput, assessing themselves in their known context, must have considered themselves physically imposing, influential, important. Then Gulliver showed up. And in our trivial pocket of reality, Gulliver is Death.

But if there *is* a "Fifth Dimension" to our existence beyond the material, if there exists a Creator who invited us into existence and has expectations of us beyond values that can be quantified, then we have an *incalculable value*. And *if*—beyond the value humanity gives us over other animals—if this Creator loves us, if this Creator wants us to live forever, in joy, then what other response is there to our lives than simply: "WOW!" And perhaps, "Thank you!" Eucharist.

Therefore, the root question of this week is, how large will you *allow* Reality to be? How can we become aware we've lost our way and the lives we're living are too *shallow?*

How capacious is the Matrix/Web/Background in which we value ourselves? When inquirers asked Jesus how they could achieve "eternal life," that's what they were asking. When anyone searches out "God's Plan," that's the outline they're searching for. What is the true meaning of "success/fulfillment/happiness"? Why are those always in the *future?*

Believers who have faced the mature crisis of childish faith presume such a matrix. Unfortunately, those who offer Christianity to the uninitiated take it for granted their audiences share their perspective and the values that outlook offers. But far too many simply don't. They've been brought up in a universe limited to *Jersey Shore,* and *Survivor*, and *Antiques Roadshow*, where anything old validates itself only with a price tag. They are utterly unaware that, in the Really Real, the money in their wallets is actually Monopoly money. Our mission is to a new foreign country in which no one can give them a motive for learning other than a certificate to make more Monopoly money.

For a great many, "holy" has no value. We offer real estate in an imaginary country no more real or accessible than Wonderland or Oz or Shangri-La.

7. THE NEVER-ENDING SUPPER

Yom Chamishi—Thursday

Later in the week, instead of going to the Temple, Jesus sent Peter and John from Bethany into the city with puzzling instructions. They were to be sure the room he'd arranged for the Passover meal would be ready for that evening.

"Just inside the Essene Gate you'll see a man carrying a pitcher of water. Follow him into the house he enters and tell the owner, 'The teacher told us to look at the upstairs room where he'll eat Passover with his men.' Get things ready for a Passover meal tonight. Judas will give you the money. But don't tell anyone where. No one. I'd like it to be a surprise."

The instructions were bewildering because it was two days before Passover, which fell that year on the Sabbath. Jerusalem lambs wouldn't be officially slaughtered till next afternoon (Friday), the Day of Preparation. But by the time they ate this meal, after sundown, it would really be Preparation Day. In a way. As for the niceties, back in Galilee, far from the Temple, they were used to killing their own lambs for the feast. But why the two of them? Judas usually took care of such things. Why not let Judas find the place? But they went. Even though they'd never find a *man* carrying a pitcher, nor even a skin bag of water.

Judas was just as puzzled, and a bit testy, when they asked for the money to buy the lamb and the bitter herbs: endive, chicory, watercress, sorrel, dandelion, horseradish. And enough wine for three shared cups. Where? Peter and John told him they had no idea yet.

In a way, all the subterfuge made sense. There had been no public warrant or threat, but any fool knew Jesus was a wanted man. They all tried not to think much about the fact that merely knowing him put their own safety in jeopardy. They were plain, simple men. Not accustomed to being noteworthy. Or even noticed.

But they found things just as Jesus had told them. A large room with tables they could push together, if that's what he wanted, and couches with cushions to recline "the Greek way" for a special feast. The host guaranteed the entire house would be free of the leaven that meant human weakness, and the lamb they had purchased would be spitted and roasted for them. It was all arranged.

That evening the Twelve drifted in along the Bethany road, around the southern wall above the Hinnom Valley, and through the Essene Gate. The first ones upstairs looked around. The tables and divans were arranged in a U-shape so all could cross-talk, but the women could access all the places from the front. Jesus, of course, would recline up at the center, but the first arrivals began to nudge one another aside somewhat impolitely as they gravitated up center. "I got here first!" and "You were the last one he picked!" and "That couch is too short for me!" None of them thought to say, "No, no, you go ahead."

In the midst of all the bickering, Jesus walked in with Peter and John who had arranged the peculiar feast. Judas followed behind, last. Jesus clapped his hands, and they all went suddenly silent. He chuckled, a bit sadly, "You've gotten it all upside down again, haven't you? About pecking order? We're not Pharisees, are we? Don't you remember the very first time you got into this foolishness? You made me laugh, right out loud! And I picked up a baby and held him up. And I said, 'See! There's what the first looks like!'

And you don't remember the story about taking the place farthest from the host? So he'll ask you to come up closer?" He shook his head, grinning. "Just stand at whatever couch you're nearest right now. We'll sing the psalm."

They tried to comply, not without a bit of elbowing in the process. This time they were all trying to get the places farthest from the center, to prove they'd listened. Judas chose the place nearest the door to the stairs.

Jesus began the Hillel psalm and his men stood awkwardly singing, like penitent boys.

"Oh, praise the Lord! You servants, praise his name!
From this time to forevermore. From sunrise to sunset,
across the heavens and above the heads of the nations!
Sing: 'Who is like the Lord our God, enthroned on high?
His eyes pierce heaven and down through all the earth!
He lifts the shattered and the lowly from the ash heap
and sits them with princes, with governors and priests.
He opens his arms to the barren and makes them fruit-
ful! Praise the Lord!'"

He poured the first cup, the cup of remembrance, and passed it to the others. "'I will bring you out,'" he quoted. "'I will open your way to freedom.'"

"Just sit on the ends first," Jesus called back as he went to the water jug and basins in the corner, put there for rinsing themselves from the road dust. He dropped his cloak in the corner, poured water into the basins, and wrapped the towel around his waist. The men shuffled and shrugged, wondering what he was up to. Jesus came to the one in the last place, the farthest from center and from the door, and knelt before him.

"How my heart has yearned to come to this moment," he said. He slipped off the sandals and took the calloused foot in his hands, splashing it with the water in the basin, wiping it with his hands, drying it with the towel. Then the other foot. "So much you don't remember. But maybe you'll remember what I'm doing right now." He moved to the next. "The learner isn't greater than the teacher, is he?"

They all mumbled, sort of meaning "No."

"Then I hope you'll remember what I do tonight."

He looked up fondly at the next one, slipped off the sandals, and picked up the foot. Each man was embarrassed, wanting to pull back. This just wasn't right. That he should act like a house slave and remove their grime, as if they were noble-blooded and he in bondage to them.

"I know you do remember that every spring," Jesus said as he worked, "we celebrate our great liberation. From slavery and humiliation. When God brought us out with his outstretched arm and strong hands from Egypt. Well, this moment begins another great rescue. Rescue from the need to be superior. And I kneel here to offer you a new covenant, a new promise."

He edged over to the next feet and slipped off the sandals. "If the loveless world hates you, remember: they hated me first. If you belonged to that world, they'd hug you in their arms. But what I'm doing now? They just won't understand. And the world hates what it can't own, can't control. So they'll hate you, hate me, hate my Father."

He edged further and looked up at Simon Peter, who seemed more frightened than when the Teacher had told him he could step out of the boat onto the stormy water.

"No, Teacher. Please," Simon stammered. "You don't want to wash my feet."

"But I really do, Simon. Remember John on the bank of the Jordan. Someday you'll be able to understand."

"Never. It's not fitting."

Jesus sank back onto his heels. "If not, you can never fit in with me."

Peter's eyes were rimmed with tears of frustration. "Yes, then. All right. And not just my feet, then, but my hands, too! And my foolish head!"

Jesus patted his knee and chuckled. "You're clean, Simon. But . . . not all of you are."

At that remark they began to bustle and buzz, but Jesus got up and changed the water. He came back and knelt and began the ritual again. Moving along the outside of the tables.

"Do you realize what I'm doing?" he asked. "You call me 'Teacher' and 'Sir' and 'Lord.' All well and good. That's who we are to one another. But the role of the true teacher, the lord, the master, is to serve. Serve the least worthy. To take away their grime, their sorrow, their fears. *That* is the lesson to remember. What I'm doing makes us entirely different. We don't scramble for the first places. We wash one another's feet. Don't just remember this. Do it. For me.

"You all listen to my voice stir the air. But not all of you truly hear." He sat back on his heels again, almost finished, suddenly sad. "I tell you truly, one of you is ready to betray me."

His words hung in the air like a dark spirit. A wave of whispers surged round the tables. "What?" . . . "Who'd dare?" . . . "I swear! Not me!" . . . "Not one of us. Not after . . ." Simon Peter, despite his conviction of innocence, remembered once when Jesus had called him "you Satan." He knuckled the man next to him, John, and said, "Ask him who. Ask him!"

But Jesus said quietly, "I'll not shame him," and pushed the bowl to the final pair of feet. He looked up into the eyes of Judas. A cluster of painful messages moved back and forth between those two pairs of eyes. A conflict of light and darkness, within each of them.

Jesus carefully bathed Judas's feet and wiped them. Then he took the basin of brown water and the soiled towel back to the corner with the water jar and returned to his place at the center. He poured the second cup, the cup of freedom from bondage, and handed it round. "'I will save you from your captors,'" he prayed.

"Now is the Son of Man glorified," he said, almost exultant.

"The time has become ripe. The seed that fell into the ground is ready to be harvested."

He stood at the head of his couch and reached for the large piece of flat bread on the plate before him, and said the blessing: "'*Barukh attah Adonai Eloheynu Melek*…Blessed are you, O Lord our God, King of Ages, who brings forth bread from the earth.'" He looked around the tables and tore the bread in half, looking from face to face. "Look at this," he said. "This is my body, broken for you. Take it and eat. Do this again and again yourselves so I may stay with you."

He passed the pieces to his right and left, and they tore off pieces for themselves, then passed them on. Wondering. Silent. Confused. Something more than a meal was happening.

Then he poured the third cup, the cup of redemption and held it up. "'*Barukh attah Adonai, Eloheynu, Melekh ha-olam, borei p'riy ha-gafen* . . . Blessed are You, Lord, our God, King of the Universe, who creates the fruit of the vine.' All of you. Look at this. This is a cup of my blood, the blood that ratifies the new covenant I now make with you. Drink it."

What were they to think? He'd changed water into wine. They'd tasted it. He'd raised the dead. He'd silenced an angry storm at sea with only a word. And he'd actually said, "If you don't eat the flesh of the Son of Man, and drink his blood, you have no true life in yourselves." They did remember that. Some wished now they hadn't.

Instead of passing the cup, he carried it to each one, starting from the far end, away from the door, and gave it to each to sip. Then, as he had on his knees, he moved to the next. And finally he came to Judas, who took the cup and drank, looking over the rim into Jesus' eyes. Jesus whispered to him so softly no one else could hear. "Do what you believe you must."

Judas hesitated. Only a moment. Then he handed back the cup, turned, and headed to the stairs. The others were too preoccupied with their own confusions even to notice he'd gone.

Night had fallen.

Jesus moved back to his place and set down the cup. "I'm going to show you," he said, "the absolute depths of my love for you. And very soon. I'm going away," he said. All of them were too jolted even to object or deny him.

"Friends, I'm only with you a little bit longer. No. You can't come this time. It's not that kind of journey. In order to give you my Spirit, I have to go. So I'm leaving you like the master in so many of the stories, with orders to take care of the vineyard while I seem gone. And here are my only orders...my *only* orders: Love one another. And not just word-love. I want you to love one another *the way I've loved you*! Always forgiving. Always starting over. If you remember *nothing* else, remember that: Love!"

Simon Peter, of course, spoke up, biting his lip. "Teacher, where?"

"You can't come with me this time. Not yet. Later, though. For sure."

But Peter couldn't let it go. No place existed where he couldn't follow. "Why not, Teacher? You know I'd give up my life for you. Like *that*!" He snapped his thick fingers.

"Really?" Jesus smiled. "Give up your life, Simon? Ah, my great-hearted friend! Before the rooster crows this very morning, you'll deny you ever knew me. More than once."

Simon's jaw dropped, unable even to stammer. As if his heart had tripped over his feet.

"But your *faith* won't fail, Simon," Jesus said. "It's rooted deep, deep in your heart. And when you come through, you'll know how to help your brothers start back, too."

Jesus kept on. "My good friends, don't let your hearts be troubled. Trust God. Trust me. I'll be right here. Not really. But *really*. That's why you have to love one another. For me. While I open the way to where my Father lives. I won't leave you orphaned! I'll come back. So you can always be with me. But by now, you do already know the way!"

Thomas, the logical, practical one, shrugged, "But, Teacher, if we don't know *where* you're going, how can we hope to find the way to it?"

Jesus splayed his hands on his big chest. "*Here*, Thomas! *I'm* the way!" Jesus said. "I'm the way. And the truth. And the way to being so alive that we'll cheat death! The way I'm going, the way to the Father is through me. If you've really known me, then you've known the Father, all along. You do know the Father. You've seen the Father!"

Poor always-baffled Philip pinched up his face trying to accommodate that. "Teacher, just *show* us the Father! Then we'll all be satisfied. Really. Once and for all."

Jesus shook his head yet again, chuckling. "Oh, Philip! After three years? And you still don't know who I really am? If you'd known me, you'd have known the Father. Truly. I told you before. The Father and I are one."

The cleverer ones scowled. They'd surely misheard again. The rest hadn't the slightest notion what he was talking about.

"What I say and do comes through me from the Father. Can you trust that I'm in the Father and the Father's in me? If that's too much, can you trust these last three years?

"I give you my solemn word. Whoever truly trusts in me will do all you've seen me doing. Greater! Because whatever you ask the Father in my name, I'll be right there with him. I'll do it. Whatever you ask in my name. I'll do it.

"You'll be less confused when the Defender comes. The Spirit of life and truth I'll send into you, who comes from the Father and who'll testify on my behalf—to ignite the wisdom and courage in you. So you can keep going and testify all you remember from our beginning together. This Spirit is beyond the grasp of even the wiliest worldlings. Because she can't be seen or weighed or bought. You've known the Spirit when you've known me. Like me, she lives in you, and will always be the fire in you.

"I'm trying to get you ready to stand on your own. But not alone. Never alone. Not too long now, and the world won't see me anymore, but you will. I'll be the life and the light and the love in you that lets you see. Only one rule: Love God by loving your neighbor, unselfishly."

Plucky Jude, the one they'd nicknamed Thaddeus the Braveheart, poked up his hand. "Teacher, why do you open yourself up to us, but not to the whole world?"

"Because, Jude, the world can't hear anything but the words. And the words and laws are just husks without the Spirit inside them, the love that brings them alive. Alive with God's life. Their lives are so full of things, there's no room for God. But you will be hollowed out. So the Father can come and find space to make his home within you. I'm telling you this based on his divine guarantee.

"All I'm saying now seems too much, too soon, but I have so little time left. No need to worry. The Helper, the Holy Spirit, the Defender, whom my Father will send in my name, will explain it all, slowly bring back all I've said and done into your remembrance—just as we remembered, always, the words and deeds of the great Moses.

"I want to leave you in peace. True peace. Not the world's peace of being unbothered, secure, complacent. I want you to find the peace that comes from honest minds and hearts, the confident peace of the tightrope walkers in caravans. Confident that I've chosen you, that if I go away it's so I can come back and never have to leave you again.

"This is how it'll be with us, always. Think of me as the vine, and you're the branches that let you drink your true life, your eternal life, through me. My Father's the gardener. He prunes away the sucker branches so the vine can be more fruitful. You're safe now, so stay connected to me, and I'll always refresh your life. If people reject their grafting into me, their spirits will die, and they'll dry up and drop away.

"The Father loves me, and I pass that love into you, like the vine to the grapes. If you keep my command, if you keep loving, no matter how bleak and impossible life becomes, you'll live, with God's life living inside your spirits.

"What I mean by 'love' is the way *I've* loved *you*. Patiently. Ready to lay down my life so you can truly live. No surer love than that. You're not my servants anymore. You're my friends. Don't let yourselves be cowed. They're going to excommunicate you. In fact, there'll come a time when some truly believe that killing you removes a deadly disease—an act of healing that pleases God. Because they misunderstand the Father—and me. When the time comes that you need it, the Defender will help you remember."

He sat down heavily at the head of his couch and let out his breath. "There are so many things I still want you to remember," Jesus said. But you're not strong enough yet to take them, flat on. But the Defender will come. The Spirit of truth. Who'll make it clear as sunlight how hollow the world's values really are before the face of my Father. *Then* you'll hear—then the ears of your ears will be opened, and you'll hear the Father as I hear him. So that the joy of your lives will be a judgment on the world's shallowness.

"Not too long now. You won't see me. Then, in a day or two, you'll always see me."

They were all at sixes and sevens, screwing up their weathered faces, afraid to ask him straight out. "He's off again . . . here, not here? . . . Day or two? . . . Is this parables again?"

"I'm confusing you again," Jesus said. "What I'm trying to tell you is too big for words. I give you my solemn word. Your confusion right now is just the beginning of your confounding. I'm trying to get you ready for grief, mourning that will seem bottomless. But it's not. For a mother in labor, the agony seems endless. But it's not. Really. And when her child breaks free, the joy of that new vibrant life is so great she can hardly remember the anguish that made it possible. Very, very soon, your spirits will be crushed with grief. But when you look back, it'll seem like only moments before your spirits erupted with joy! And nobody—nobody—can ever take that joy out of your hearts. Then, you'll be beyond questions. Beyond fear. Once you're reborn!

"For so long, I've had to try explaining the truly real to you in a roundabout way, trying to explain what you don't understand from things you do. That's the best anybody could do. But when the Spirit opens your minds—and hearts—then we can speak to you about the Father flat out, and you'll know us not in the words but in *one another*. Because the Father loves you, in a special way, because you've loved me. I came from the Father, into this world. And now, my good friends, I'm leaving the world to go back to my Father."

"Ah!" a few of them sighed. "All right! That's straight talk. We know it now for sure."

"Of course, we know you come from God."

"I never doubted that. Hardly ever."

Jesus' smile slowly waned. "So, now, you believe. But," he said, "the hour—the appointed time—is coming. No. It's here. You'll all run. No, don't look so surprised. You will. To save your own skins. You'll leave me alone, deserted. I may feel abandoned, but I'm never really alone. I trust my Father is always with me. I'm telling you all this so you'll take heart, so you won't let your failures last. So you'll turn back home. Like the boy from his swine. You'll have troubles in the godless world. But hold your chins up! I'm here to frustrate that world."

Jesus raised his eyes and began to pray, quietly, but they could hear. "Father, it's time. Let your glory shine out through your Son as a testimony to you. Just as you entrusted me with all human flesh so I could pass on to them the life that's in us. So they can feel the real, eternal life pulsing in their spirits. So they can grasp what they were born for—eternal life, knowing you, with every intensity, the one true God. And Jesus the Christ whom you've sent.

"I've glorified you here by fulfilling all you asked of me. Now, I pray, raise me back up with you, to share again the glory we've shared since before there was a world. I opened your will to these men and women you gave me, and they've stayed true—even though they have to trust my word that it is true. They believe—as far as they can come so far. All that they are is now yours. They now contain what I've been for them and for you.

"I don't belong here any longer. But they have to keep going, here. As I leave them, hold them close. Help them swallow their peevishness so they blend into one, as you and I are one. As I've tried so hard to keep them together. Except for the one.

"I'm coming home to you. And I want to fill them with the joy that can face down the world, to tempt the world to turn and find real life. I don't ask that you take them from the world, but that you make them ours—sacred, out of the reach of Evil. Protected by their firm grasp on your truth, as I have been. I go forward into the terrifying glory so they may share it.

"I don't pray just for them. I beg that you keep loving watch also on the ones who believe in what I've brought them, believe because of the belief and witness of my friends here with me now. I pray that all of them, from now through forever, can be fused into one new people, knowing and loving one another and us. So that, unto forever, they may embody the love we have shared since before the beginning."

They'd gone past midnight. He closed his eyes for a moment. Then he stood.

"It's time," he said.

Puzzling Moments

Insolubles

(1) John has no explicit record of the institution of the Eucharist. It's puzzling that he would purposely omit it. Especially because only John shows Jesus insisting that "the bread that I will give for the life of the world is my flesh" (6:51). That assertion was enough to make some of the disciples break with him.

(2) Along the same line, so many good-hearted priests and laypeople have imposed an absolute precision in the words of consecration over the years, as if they were some kind of voodoo imposition on the power of God. Although the three Synoptics and St. Paul agree on the general intention of the words of consecration, none of them is a meticulous mirror-image of any of the others. Again, on a matter so "crucial," the nonagreement is puzzling, but also reassuring.

—Matthew: While they were eating, Jesus took a loaf of bread, and after blessing it he broke it, gave it to the disciples, and said, *"Take, eat; this is my body."* Then he took a cup, and after giving thanks he gave it to them, saying, *"Drink from it, all of you; for this is my blood of the covenant, which is poured out for many for the forgiveness of sins"* (26:26-28).

— Mark: While they were eating, he took a loaf of bread, and after blessing it he broke it, gave it to them, and said, *"Take; this is my body."* Then he took a cup, and after giving thanks he gave it to them, and all of them drank from it. He said to them, *"This is my blood of the covenant, which is poured out for many"* (14:22-24).

—Luke: Then he took a loaf of bread, and when he had given thanks, he broke it and gave it to them, saying, *"This is my body, which is given for you.* Do this in remembrance of me." And he did the same with the cup after supper, saying, *"This cup that is poured out for you is the new covenant in my blood"* (22: 19-20).

—Paul: The Lord Jesus on the night when he was betrayed

took a loaf of bread, and when he had given thanks, he broke it and said, *"This is my body that is for you.* Do this in remembrance of me."* In the same way he took the cup also, after supper, saying, *"This cup is the new covenant in my blood.* Do this, as often as you drink it, in remembrance of me."* As often as you eat this bread and drink the cup, you proclaim the Lord's death until he comes (1 COR 11:27-29).

(3) Although both Luke and Paul separate the two consecrations and explicitly say the cup was consecrated "after supper," none of the sources—not one—says anything about the actual Hebrew meal itself, or the lamb, or who prepared and served it. So neither did I.

One answer that really ought to satisfy anyone with a transcendent perspective is that, to those who chose what to write in their Gospels and, presumably their audiences, such precisions were just *not* important. Threat of arrest and martyrdom does amplify one's viewpoint radically.

Beyond argument, the intention outweighed any "formula."

Day of the Week

Scottish biblical scholar F. F. Bruce called this question "the thorniest problem in the New Testament." Most readers might say the resurrection tops that, but to a specialist the question is quite real. All four Gospels agree Jesus died on our Friday and that they celebrated a "special" meal the previous evening. But magnifying-glass inspection shows quite a few mismatching patches.

Twenty-five percent of Matthew's book is Holy Week, 30 percent of Mark, 20 percent of Luke, and almost 40 percent of John. The Last Supper, arguably the most famous meal in history, a happening repeated day after day, century after century, is four rough sketches, not clear-cut blueprints.

John has Jesus' death explicitly on "Preparation Day," which for the knowing Jewish converts would have the dramatic coincidence of Jesus' death at the very moment nearly a quarter-million Passover lambs were being slaughtered in the nearby Temple. Then his burial was hurried to avoid Passover. The three Synoptics begin the Last Supper segment with: "On the first day [of seven] of Unleavened Bread, when the Passover lamb is sacrificed." Since the lamb was then taken to eat at the evening meal (the Jewish day began at first starlight, not midnight or dawn), this would have the supper on the *day* of Passover—adding the significance of Jesus' death as the moment when Yahweh set free the Hebrew slaves. But if Good Friday were the Passover day, the chief priests could not have bought the Potter's Field, nor could Joseph of Arimathea buy linen, nor would Simon of Cyrene do field work. It was unlawful to buy, sell, or work during Passover.

A more down-to-earth difficulty is the number of events and their duration which all the four writers cram into too brief a time. All agree that the Last Supper was a leisurely meal (in John five chapters, nine full pages) which likely went on well after midnight. If Jesus died at three the following afternoon, one has to imagine that thirteen hours is sufficient time for the half-hour rocky walk to the Mount of Olives, what appears to be some intense time of Jesus in agonized prayer, and whatever time it took to effect his arrest and walk him down the hill, across the valley, across the entire width of the city to the house of Annas (only John), then down the street to Caiaphas the High priest—who had apparently already rousted the seventy other Sanhedrin members from their beds (along with the inconstant "witnesses").

Like all narratives of courtroom activities, the ensuing accounts of the Jewish interrogation and the later multiple encounters with the vacillating Pilate, not to mention Pilate's attempt to shift the burden by sending Jesus to Herod (only Luke)—all were done not at a breakneck, efficient pace but with the leisurely self-indulgence of pampered, self-important men.

Sometime in that early morning the Roman soldiers had time to mock and buffet Jesus, and to carry out Pilate's orders to scourge him—thirty-nine times, one lash short of death. Then, after Jesus was condemned, it took quite some time to boot him through the narrow streets, sagging underneath the crossbar, falling at times and slowing at every pace. Then the business of spiking him to the bar, hoisting him up onto the upright pole, then waiting impatiently for him to give up.

Biblical scholars have crisscrossed Jerusalem with stopwatches, pausing for what their educated guesses assessed the time each event might have consumed, and concluded that any meticulous literal reading of any Gospel, or all four uneasily harmonized, was simply impossible.

Using different time reckonings (from midnight or from dawn at six), Mark is easily misread as showing Jesus crucified at nine, but John at noon. The writers were not likely to have forgotten when in the day Jesus was executed. Therefore, they used different reckonings.

Not only was there more than one accepted method of designating days of the week and the division of a day's hours, there were a number of different Jewish calendars in use in Israel in the first century CE. Thus, different Jewish groups celebrated Passover on different days, just as today Catholics, Protestants, and variants of Orthodox Christianity differ on the date of Easter.

Sir Colin Humphreys, a physicist at Cambridge University, utilizing the full gamut of biblical, historical, and even astronomical sources, finds a tempting solution in merely pushing our Holy Thursday back to the Wednesday—which all four Gospels leave "empty," like an extra Sabbath that week—which would have been disturbingly anxious hours, given the impending peril.

That would mean a shift in lifelong convictions about days now immovably "sacred." But belief in what transpires at the

Eucharist ought hardly to pivot on which weekday it first occurred.

In *A Marginal Jew*, John Meier offers another possible scenario, one quite plausible with any reading of the Gospel tradi-
tion:

> Sensing or suspecting that his enemies were closing in for
> an imminent, final attack, and therefore taking into ac-
> count that he might not be able to celebrate the coming
> Passover meal with his disciples, Jesus instead arranged a
> solemn farewell meal with the inner circle of disciples just
> before Passover.

No need to clutter the reader's mind here with the minute
details. In 2007, Pope Benedict XVI *suggested* that Jesus might
have used the solar calendar of the Essenes of Qumran.

"Let the day's own trouble be sufficient for the day" (MT 6:34).

Where?

Just as there "were" once nearly a dozen heads of John the
Baptist in shrines all over Europe (detached, some averred, at
different times of his life), no one is death-and-taxes sure of
where in present-day Jerusalem the Last Supper took place. And
unlike Greece or Rome, anywhere in the Holy Land even vaguely reputed to be a sacred locale has had a cathedral heaped up on
top of it, just as baffled Peter wanted to do at the transfiguration.
Some claim the householder was Nicodemus, Joseph of Arimathea, the mother of John Mark. The truth is, no one knows.
But while speculation on slim evidence is justifiably *verboten* in
the academy, it does little harm for someone trying prayerfully to
"decompact" the event and relive it.

Some of the details at least tempt a reader to modify the location from "somewhere in the city." One is the trivial detail of a
man carrying a pitcher of water. Drawing water was "women's
work," and they carried it from the well in jugs and pitchers. If
men were forced to carry water, it was in leather bags for travel.

Essenes were in every Jewish town and known for their hospitality. But Essenes were celibate and had no women to do such chores, and the gate at the southwestern corner of the Jerusalem wall was "the Essenes' Gate."

What tickles the imagination is to imagine the New Passover transpiring just up the street from the mansions of Annas and Caiphas, who will that day deliver up its Host for sacrifice.

A Passover Seder?

Virtually all experts agree that, as a Jew, Jesus would have observed Jewish rituals as they were practiced *in his day*. But abundant evidence shows the seder has evolved over the centuries, and much of what Jews today presume at the seder table would have been unknown to Jesus and his fellow Jews in ancient Jerusalem.

In Luke, at the supper, Jesus says, "I have eagerly desired to eat this Passover" (22:15). For that reason, I have interpolated references and words not in evidence in the Gospels (which I've done all along) to suggest the mood of the event. But, as a minor for-instance, the "official" Passover meal was eaten in haste, *standing*. However, during the Last Supper Jesus and the disciples were reclining. (Depending on your translation, all four Gospels use this idea for participants at formal dining situations in occupied Palestine at the time, and there is ample evidence that such was a custom, rather than the seating imposed by da Vinci and other artists.)

As usual, theology and interpretation trump historical exactitude. Thus the Last Supper was a full fellowship meal, looking back on the exodus and immediately forward to the crucifixion and ultimately to the *parousia* (second coming) and messianic banquet/kingdom. The words recall an earlier covenant's ratification in Exodus. Somehow a new promise is being forged, and the blood Jesus shed at the hands of the Romans seals it. It is beyond denial the original writers and readers testified with their own deaths that this was their belief.

Both John Meier and N. T. Wright believe that Jesus, aware that his hours were numbered because of what he'd done so far that week, arranged a *kind-of* Passover meal, a solemn communal sharing of food to celebrate a shift in the relationship of Yahweh and People as dramatic and life changing as the exodus from historical slavery. Despite any conflict of theories, it was a Passover meal. Just no longer a Hebrew one.

Judas and the Eucharist

The "morsel" Jesus dips in the dish and hands to Judas (Jn 13:26) ought not be confused with Jesus offering him the Eucharist. If anything, it was a way Jesus used to identify who the betrayer would be. (Remember, John is the only one who declares, baldly, that Judas's motive was larceny.) Along with Augustine and Aquinas, I see a more Christlike attitude.

Luke offers a route to a more irenic insight into Jesus, even though he places a burden on the self-righteous who see "Satan entering Judas" as placing him beyond redemption. Luke says— *after* the Eucharist (22:14-20)—only in the following verse, "But see, the one who betrays me is with me, and his hand is on the table" (22:21).

In the *Summa* (Q. 81, Art. 2: "Whether Jesus gave his body to Judas"), Aquinas argues:

> Since Christ was to serve us as a pattern of justice, it was not in keeping with His teaching authority to sever Judas, a hidden sinner, from Communion with the others without an accuser and evident proof—lest the Church's prelates might have an example for doing the like, and lest Judas himself being exasperated might take occasion of sinning. Therefore, it remains to be said that Judas received our Lord's body and blood with the other disciples.

Augustine, too, writes: "It must be understood that our Lord had already distributed the sacrament of His body and blood to

all His disciples, among whom was Judas also, as Luke narrates"
(Tract. lxii in Joan.).

This large-heartedness in Jesus at least ought to suggest second thoughts to those well-meaning Catholics who wish to use denial of the Eucharist as a kind of punishment for sins that, to them, seem to place wrongdoers beyond the compassion of Christ.

Of the four, only the gentle Luke interjects the disturbing statement from Jesus that, unlike the missions where he sent them without money or even a staff, they should now equip themselves with both, and, "The one who has no sword must sell his cloak and buy one" (22:36). First of all, he's not speaking of a huge battle sword, merely the long knife any Galilean would feel naked without when on a journey. Also, in common sense, Jerusalem was a city with a reputation for murdering prophets. If nothing else, he is stressing that antagonism with the authorities is no longer merely theoretical. Unlike previous missions, they are decidedly unwelcome here.

Taken literally, this order is more in line with the righteous violence Jesus untypically used in the Temple and surely a far cry from loving your enemies and turning the other cheek. Jesus' later reaction to cutting off the servant's ear clearly shows his disciples misunderstood. When they tell Jesus they do have two "swords," he says: "That's enough." He can't possibly mean "That's sufficient," since starting a revolution with two swords and eleven untrained men is ridiculous. My unfounded hunch is Jesus meant: "Well, let's be finished with *that*."

The insertion might be to ground Jesus' cryptic appeal in Scripture: "He was counted among the lawless" (Lk 22:37), an allusion back to the Suffering Servant songs of Isaiah. That will turn out to be exactly the argument the Jewish leaders will bring to Pilate to justify his crucifixion: insurrection. This addition is quite likely Luke amplifying the resonance to the long-range Plan—if indeed Jesus said anything at all like this.

However, all along Jesus has used physical symbols (seeds, lamps, vineyards, lost coins, sheep, sons) to anchor nonphysical truths. A perfectly sound argument is that here Jesus wasn't talking about solid weapons any more than when he said, "I come to bring not peace but a sword" (MT 10:34). St. Paul, independently, may have come up with a much more satisfying *symbolic* association of physical armor with the life of the Christian:

> Therefore take up the whole armor of God . . . . Fasten the belt of truth around your waist, and put on the breastplate of righteousness . . . to proclaim the gospel of peace. With all of these, take the shield of faith, with which you will be able to quench all the flaming arrows of the evil one. Take the helmet of salvation, and the sword of the Spirit, which is the word of God. (EPH 6:14-18)

The Christian facing "arrest," like Jesus, needs a quite different armorer.

Elements to Ponder

Taking the Last Place

Humility quite often teeters on the edges of hypocrisy. Sometimes, it can actually become a mask for narcissism: arrogant humility. "I'm so far from being vain that I'm really the worst of the worst." A laughably baseless challenge to such evil paragons as Genghis Khan, Hitler, Pol Pot, and Saddam Hussein. "Hey, Jesus! Look at me! I'm *not* out there on the dance floor with the featherheads! I'm out here, up to my elbows in greasy pots at the slop sink!"

The Latin root of both "humble" and "human" is *humus*, dirt: down to earth. The greatest humility is never to lie to yourself about yourself. To have the perspective to laugh at your own pretensions. On the contrary, to say "I'm nobody" is an insult to the Host who invited us.

Peter Refuses to Be Washed

He's unique, unbending, devoted—and clueless. From the very first instant Jesus got his attention, he couldn't submit his life-long sense of unimportance to the truth that Jesus loved him—no matter what. "Go away from me, Lord. I'm a sinful man" (Lk 5:8). In a similar way, at the mere mention one would betray him, all the other apostles, even the ones who knew they were innocent, were ready to jump into the guilt swamp. "I've been tempted to leave. . . . I'm probably the dumbest. . . . Did I do something without realizing?" Despite all their misunderstandings, despite the unpleasant and even repulsive people Jesus forced them to associate with, despite even his constant scorn for their ambitions and his humbling demands, they'd stayed. But they still felt unworthy of his love and trust. Of course, they were unworthy. That's the whole point. That's what "grace" *means*: unmerited love.

Such self-effacing humility is pitifully common in good people, never far enough away from the parental voice saying, "Now don't you get *vain!*" If you don't trust the vehicle, how will it ever take you anywhere? Our Creator found no trouble making a universe out of nothing.

Not Servants but Friends

A justifiable question to adults and becoming-adults: In your one-on-one prayer, do you still "deal with" God as you did when you were a child? Or as if you were a vassal unworthy to raise your head in the presence of majesty?

Think of the liberating moment when, without planning it, you found yourself dealing with your own parents as a fellow adult. It adds a far richer—and more fitting—attitude and tone to the relationship. What would it take to rise to that unselfconscious ease with God?

I used to pray to God as "a Person made of Light." Now, long practice has made our interchanges more down to earth; I have a different, more easeful position. It's not a purposeful evocation each time, like a "composition of place." More like an attitude. Jesus and I are bumping along in the cab of his pickup. He's a sheepherder, not the wimpy Jesus of the holy cards. More like Hugh Jackman, big and with a ready grin. And he smells unmistakably of sheep. Not much I can tell him he doesn't already know. I don't "work for" him. I have a share in his "business," and he no longer has to tell me what to do. Now we pretty much read one another's minds. Not much chatter. Often, the distractions are the conversation. Although neither of us says too much, there's a real conversation going on underneath the silence. Being with. I reassure myself once again I'm never really alone. And it's exhilarating to know he enjoys being with me. No longer just "tolerates." In all honesty, I confess it sometimes takes an effort for me to admit that Jesus enjoys being with *me*. When I'm flummoxed, I edge over and lean my head on his big shoulder.

Transubstantiation

Emperor Charles V gathered representatives of Rome and each of the Protestant factions, begging them all to agree that at least *somehow* Jesus was more intensely present in the Eucharist than anywhere else on Earth. The God we believe in somehow created a universe out of nothing and somehow animated a human being with divinity. Such a God would surely have found no difficulty in fusing that same divinity into bread and wine. But, stubbornly, they refused, each nursing his own pet theory. How foolish. As foolish as trying to define strictly when and how love is present and when and how love is not.

If we can accept that the infinite God could fuse into an embryo, why would anyone balk at accepting that he could also enter—however he chose—a sliver of bread and a puddle of wine?

The Protestant theologian Karl Barth articulates what a difference it makes to believe that the presence of the risen Lord actually is not only in the gathered assembly and in God's word and in the priest but actually in the bread and wine:

> At those times when the task of being ministers of the divine word, as we of the Reformed Churches say, has oppressed us, have we not all felt a yearning for the rich services of Catholicism, and for the enviable role of the priest at the altar? When he elevates the *Sanctissimum*, with its full measure of that meaning and power which the *material* symbol enjoys over the symbol of the human word, the double grace of the sacrificial death and the incarnation of the Son of God is not only preached in words but actually takes place in his hands.

Until you can feel within yourself that experience of the reality of death and the reality of rebirth, you will never feel the reality of the Lord's Supper, even when it is well performed.

In her magnificent chronicle, *The Man on a Donkey*, H. F. M. Prescott explains the Eucharist better than any systematic theologian I've ever encountered:

> He came stilly as rain, and even now cometh into the darkness of our bellies—God in a bit of bread, to bring morning into our souls.

And another novelist, Flannery O'Connor, wrote just as crisply: "If it's just a symbol, then I say t'hell with it."

A Meditation

Once on a retreat, my director suggested I meditate on Jesus washing the apostles' feet. It was the sixth day, and I was pretty much retreated-out. But, dutifully, I tried. Empty and dry as a Saharan savannah. But a Presence crept up on me and gave me a hint. Instead of, humbly, inhabiting one of the embarrassed disciples, cringing as Jesus knelt his way toward me, I boldly inhabited Jesus, on my knees with a basin and towel.

But the Presence snookered me. When I looked up, the men around the table were the Jesuits of my own community at the time. I knelt in front of the first and said to myself, "Of course, I'll wash your feet. It's a privilege." Then I hunched over to the next, looked up and said, "Sure." And so it went. But then came the surprise, the epiphany. I looked up and said, through my teeth, "I'll be *damned* if I'll wash your feet!"

It gave me a lasting insight into my own claim to humility. It also gave me a profounder understanding of the difference between "like" and "love."

8. The Hour of the Power of Darkness

Yom Shishi: Friday, Past Midnight

It was very early in the morning. Everything had gone quiet. They left the upper room through full-moon-shadowed streets, out the Essene Gate. The rocky path was so narrow and steep along the dark city wall from the gate to Olivet Hill, they could walk only single file and couldn't hear Jesus. So he had them sing the other Hallel psalms. Softly, not to call attention.

> What can I possibly return to the Lord
> for the kindness he has poured out to me?
> I will raise high the cup of salvation,
> a toast lifted to the name of the Lord!
> I will keep the promises I made him,
> an offering before all his people.
> Precious in his eyes are the deaths of his faithful.
> I have been your servant, Lord, freely.
> I offer you the sacrifice of thanks
> and call on the holy name of the Lord.
> I completed all that I promised to do.
> I offer it in the presence of all your people,
> in Jerusalem, the city of God. Praise the Lord!

Peter was right next to Jesus and just couldn't let it go. "Teacher, my word on it! Even if every one of the others deserts, I won't. I promise!"

Jesus wasn't smiling. He merely said, "Before cockcrow, Simon. Three times."

Peter growled, "I'll *die* first!"

And those closest mumbled the same thing.

They left the path along the southern wall above the Hinnom Valley and broke out into full moonlight up along the dry Kidron stream bed. They could extinguish and throw away their few feeble torches. They climbed quietly up through the encampment of pilgrims, into the olive trees, then into an open grove where Jesus often took them to pray. The rough grass among the trees was patched with moonlight, and tiny clusters of white blossoms poked through the long silvered leaves. He gestured for them to find places, and said, "Sit here awhile. I need to pray."

He gestured to Peter, James, and John to follow a little more closely. He went a stone's throw further and signaled for the three to sit at the thick trunk of a very old olive tree. "Pray with me," he said, nervously, clearly distressed. "I'm scared to death. Stay with me?"

He moved a bit farther off and threw himself to his knees, his arms straight and stiff at his sides. Then, suddenly, he jerked forward, as if he'd been struck in the stomach. They could barely make out his words.

"Papa. My Father! Please!" he gasped. "You can do anything. Take this cup of wrath away. I beg you. But . . . I know. I know. What I want is so small compared to what you want." He knelt there a long while. Helpless. Murmuring. In the silence, their attention wandered.

After a long while, Jesus heaved to his feet and walked back to his three closest friends. What with the hour and the wine, they'd fallen asleep.

Jesus nudged Simon's foot with his toe, and the man jerked awake, jarring the heads of the other two from his shoulders.

"Simon? Not even an hour? Pray with me that you don't enter the contest flat-footed. Stay with me. Please."

He went back and fell down again. "My Father, there *must* be an easier way. Please. I never could have imagined it would be this ugly. This shameful. Please." He kept mumbling, gutted with revulsion. He fell silent. Gradually, his breath calmed and he lurched to his feet.

Again, they'd been unable to keep their eyes open. They jumped when he touched them, shamefaced. "I know," Jesus said. "The spirit is willing; the flesh is weak."

He moved away and dropped to his knees, praying the same "if only" words. Finally, his head jerked up at the faint smell of burning pitch, and he looked off toward the city wall where a thin line of fire had begun to ease up the hillside below them.

He ached to his feet and moved back to the special three and shook them. The one who had said he'd die rather than leave him. The brothers who'd sworn they could drink the cup and stand on either side of him in glory. They awoke groggily and dumbly followed him to the others. As those woke, they were muzzy, embarrassed, like sentries or pupils caught dozing.

"Wake up, friends! Wake up!" Jesus called to them with a hollow cheerfulness, and they murmured and pawed up out of heavy sleep. "The turncoat's here. It's the time. Be brave!"

And there the Enemy stood just outside the grove. Uniformed Temple police with torches and batons, and other nighthawks they must have picked up along the way. Some priests stood safely behind them.

And at the head of them was Judas, their brother.

Puzzling Moments

A Garden

The garden is, of course, symbolic. Jesus was never savaged by doubts by daylight, in the Temple or even out in the wilderness, as in his first true temptations. Here, he faces the Power of Darkness in the early hours of the morning, in a garden. The first symbolic conflict with Evil had been in a garden, when Adam and Eve challenged the preeminence of God. Now, within one human being, the spirits of Light and Darkness contend to the death. And Magdalene will encounter the triumphant risen Jesus in yet another garden.

The Cup

The cup is a frequent OT symbol for "the wrath of God," as in Psalm 75:8: "For in the hand of the Lord there is a cup, and the wine is red; it is full of corruptions; and he poureth out of the same: but the dregs thereof, all the wicked of the earth shall wring them out, and drink them." And Jeremiah 25:15-16: "The Lord God of Israel saith unto me: 'Take the wine cup of this fury at my hand, and cause all the nations, to whom I send thee, to drink it. And they shall drink, and be moved, and be mad." Isiaah 51:17, 22: "O Jerusalem, which hast drunk at the hand of the Lord the cup of his fury; thou hast drunken the dregs of the cup of trembling, and wrung them out. . . . Behold, I have taken out of thine hand the cup of trembling, even the dregs of the cup of my fury; thou shalt no more drink it again."

All along, I've contested the validity of the atonement metaphor in the face of the evidence of Jesus' concrete practice with sinners. Anthropomorphism often attributes human weaknesses to a God who, by definition, can't even be upset. The staggering truth of the incarnation is that God actually, freely, submitted— for the first time (at least that we know of)—not just to the humiliations that the humanized animal must submit to, but to the bitterest "dregs" of God's "wrath."

Wrath is easy to grasp because we share fear, the lowest of motives, with other animals who lack the grace of human perspective. On the other hand, only humans can be aware of being "wicked," conscious of missing the point of our specific, divinely designed nature (our programing). No rock despairs and implodes, no cabbage refuses nourishment, no lemming commits suicide. (They're just too dumb to sense how far they can swim.) But humans do "blow up," we refuse to feed our minds and hearts, we do despair and quit the (human) race. We do sin; we do violate the invitations of our nature and thereby insult our Benefactor. Even if our Creator had made us with no expectations of "reward" to him, our scandalous lack of gratitude would be one more insult, added to the guilt of misusing his gifts. Because we have the intelligence to realize our giftedness, we *ought* to crave the chance to be honorable and rectify it.

Stripped of "the economic metaphor," then, Jesus did take into himself responsibility for all our self-centeredness, our stupidities, our cowardice. And he "drank" it to the dregs.

What does "the cup" mean, then? Again, given Jesus' attitude toward sinners, it *can't* mean *retributive* suffering. More likely it means *redemptive* suffering—not redeeming a debt to a hostile lender but offering us a second chance, freeing us from the ballast of guilt and opening the opportunity to get on with it again. (According to Jesus: "Seventy times seven times" chances.) If only we would wake up from our teflon cocoons and accept the invitation.

The cup is an *invitation* (a metaphor light-years away from wrathful retribution) to swallow one's pride. Just as before I challenged the Dantean metaphors of a purgatory of physical torment, I'd appeal again to the higher-level metaphor of dealing with a sensitive psychotherapist (soul doctor). Slowly, painfully, facing the shaming truths of our weak responses to challenge—pitifully small in contrast to the epic challenge to which Jesus rises in this Holy Week story—but still painful. Admitting that our selfish convictions were insulting and arrogant, that we'd lost the perspective of the Really Real, that—like the first dumb humans in Eden and the first Chosen People for centuries—we had acted as if we were capable of happiness in the absence of God.

Again, we encounter the Plan. Even accepting that God's plan for human beings is not a detailed map or a blueprint or a rigid plot outline, even granted that the Plan is that there's no plan, that the premise is a life of improvisation in a world where the unexpected is the only thing we can expect, what possible reason could a sensible God have in creating a life that inevitably, constantly, sometimes overwhelmingly throws up obstacles and frustrations? WHY?

Could a powerful clue lie in placing our own lifelong challenges into the perspective of the continuing growth of a universe we'd once thought was limited to where we humans happen to be? Could another clue be the glacial-but-unceasing evolution of our own earth from dead matter through endless eons to Teresa of Avila and Werner Heisenberg? Could our incessant yearning for more, that's so easily distracted into covetousness, be a suggestion—built right into what we are and where we are—that we're "born for better things"? That what will make us happy-successful-fulfilled is the *process* of enriching our minds and hearts? And that we achieve that human purpose precisely in rising to those obstacles—with dignity.

We encounter that invitation the instant we're ejected from the womb, when we're weaned, when we're abandoned at the preschool doorway. We face it when our bodies begin to betray us in adolescence, when we offer to share our newfound selves in the intimacy of marriage, in the challenges of parenthood, in the harsh truths of aging, in the inescapable encounter with death. Unending challenge *is* the Plan.

The hardships of life are not some sadistic "test" to see if we can "merit to be coheirs." It is, rather, a period of *training*. Exercises to deepen our souls and broaden our perspectives so that, eventually, we will be able to accommodate the joys of the Really Real.

Elements to Ponder

God in Agony: The Cup

The Greek word "*agonia*" is a technical term for the warm-up exercises whereby Olympian athletes stretched their muscles and lungs, worked up a sweat to be ready for the real thing. The modern ethos can't accommodate the ancient desert fathers and mothers who retired from the World to pray and deprive themselves with physical penances—just as modern monastics still do. It's unnatural, they claim, to freely impose on oneself physical mortifications to placate a vengeful God. I would agree heartily to the absurdity of the placating motive. But there is, and has always been, a universal agreement among athletes on the essential practice of "training." Wind sprints and weightlifting are painful! But they're self-imposed for a purpose: They teach a lesson to the body whereby I tell it when to quit, and it doesn't tell me.

The whole truth of the "penances" emerges when we drain the metaphor of propitiating a God who keeps scrupulous records of wrongs and "the punishments due to sin." How much more meaningful self-denial (self-control) would be if we yanked our metaphors from the hands of accountants into the hands of athletic coaches. "Penances" aren't payments to a loan shark but exercises to "improve my game," make me a better, tougher, more authentic human being.

St. Paul understood: "Athletes exercise self-control in all things; they do it to receive a perishable wreath, but we an imperishable one. So I do not run aimlessly, nor do I box as though beating the air" (1 COR 9:25-26). And the race isn't a sprint; it's a marathon. Few expect to "win" a marathon, to out-strive anyone else but themselves.

Elsewhere, I've said the major attraction in Christianity for me is that it's the only religion I know whose God was tempted simply to give up. As I have been tempted. I've also argued that this was precisely the reason for the incarnation. Not grim atonement to a terminally offended Deity but an example of how human beings can welcome and encompass the divine life they were invited to from the beginning.

This "cup" in Gethsemane—this challenge to give up, to find an easier way—had to be a real temptation to Jesus. Just as the wilderness temptations had to be. And forget the enfeebling theological distinction of "Jesus felt it *only* in his humanity." John puts the facts of it starkly, with no need for theoretical precisions: "The Word *became flesh.*" The whole point of the incarnation is that the Architect of the Universe, the God of Job (!), chose to become a helpless infant, a boy who needed his diapers changed and lessons in lacing sandals, a teacher who faced resolutely resistant students, and now, here, spectacularly, he freely submits to the worst that being human could require. He had become flesh; now "*he became sin*" (2 Cor 5:21). As an example of bringing apparent defeat into assessment before the background of the Really Real, where death is always the price of rebirth.

Experts call that background "eschatological, transcendental, theological, mythic, spiritual," a perspective that stretches beyond what we ordinarily concern ourselves with in everyday life. It puts our here-and-now struggles into a transcosmic struggle. A need for that "larger sense" is what provokes such a constant appeal of mythic tales like the Greco-Roman myths in which humans struggle with—and against—gods, Norse Eddas like Beowulf, Grimm tales of a world where wonder and enchantment haven't been smothered, battles between two radically opposed "standards" in *Star Wars, Lord of the Rings, Harry Potter.* Even old westerns and potboiler gothic novels appeal to our primal conviction that, although the two are most often very confusing in what we take for life, "Good" and "Evil" are *real*, and they've been in life-and-death conflict since humans received the powers to choose.

This was the first time *God* had *suffered.* The God who out-exists time and space—and limitations and emotions and loss—never had need to experience suffering, "in the gut." Only in the same sense well-fed academics can write papers on starvation or celibates can empathize with problems of married couples. God can look down from the cross and say, "Yes, Job. Now I do know how it feels."

The Bloody Sweat

From now on, the physical blood of Jesus will become very much a motif of the story. Participants in its unfolding will be quoted as claiming exemption from guilt for Jesus' blood: Judas, Herod, Pilate. The silver to Judas is "blood money" and will be used to purchase *Haceldema*, "The Field of Blood," a cemetery for criminals and the destitute, with whom Jesus was so intimate. Matthew will show "the people" shouting the unthinkable "his blood be upon us and our children" that has insidiously pretended to justify Semitic persecution among the small-souled to this day. More importantly, the idea of blood will be a link between this week's story and the Really Real Story: the blood with which Moses sprinkled the Hebrews to seal their Covenant, the cup Jesus shared at the supper, and the blood Jesus sheds on Calvary and offers endlessly now in the Eucharist.

As for a *literal* basis for a bloody sweat, arguments are more tenuous. First of all, the only biblical source is Luke, and the notion could be as slimly grounded as the assertion that the author of Luke's Gospel was a trained physician (COL 4:14). And that Gospel says only "his sweat became *like* great drops of blood." The text doesn't say it was blood (as the texts do say the Eucharist is) nor if it was even "tinged" with red. Leonardo da Vinci described a man who sweated blood before a battle. Some medical authorities today cite cases of "hematidrosis," in which the subcutaneous capillaries are so swollen by stress that they erupt into the sweat glands. Cases occur in modern times where bloody water leaks from noses and tear ducts. Studies in psychosomatic illness show mental anguish can trigger genuine physical trauma.

Be that as it may, are we left to assume also the physical reality of the tongues of fire and the hurricane wind of Pentecost? Must we also "postulate" a sudden sandstorm enveloping Jerusalem at the moment of Christ's death? A farther reach: Was no one else near Bethlehem but the shepherds awakened at Christ's birth when the entire heavenscape was crowded with legions of angels singing their (nonexistent) lungs out?

In his monumental work *The Death of the Messiah*, Raymond Brown, S.S., has noted, "Often the medical writers have expressed their conclusions without recognizing that any or all these features might embody *theological* symbolism rather than *historical description*." Keep remembering the valid distinction between "accurate" and "meaningful." Any attempt to ground the trustworthiness of the Pentecost "tongues of fire" by an appeal to a first-century outbreak of St. Elmo's fire in Jerusalem seems to attest a very weak faith reaching out for any flotsam after a shipwreck. After genuine faith has floundered.

Praying to Change God's Mind

This picture of the hero begging to be passed over is consistent with nearly every figure in the Old Testament like Moses and Jeremiah who pleaded with Yahweh to find someone else. But it is in stark contrast to other intrepid heroes of classical mythologies who sprang eagerly (i.e., without thinking) to struggle against gods. Jesus' pleading is a scandalous contrast to the stoic death of Socrates who went to his suicide as serenely as an old man to his afternoon nap.

Further, Jesus' story of the man knocking on the door at night (MT 7:7) says persistence in praying *will* get results. And is there a single place in the Gospels where someone came to Jesus and pleaded with genuine faith and was turned away? But most of us know you can pray for years, passionately, and come up empty-handed. In my mother's last three years, when she rarely knew me and was sometimes even terrified of me, I said Mass every day for no other intention but that God would let her go. And God didn't come through.

Since grade school, we've been given placebos like: "Oh, God will give you something even *better*" or "What you asked for really isn't the best for you" or "You probably didn't pray with enough faith." But the knocking-on-the-door parable (LUKE 11), taken by itself, doesn't allow for better substitutes. It says, if you ask for a fish, you get a fish not a snake; ask for an egg and you don't get a scorpion. Jesus also said, if you have faith no bigger than a mustard seed (tiny as a pinhead), you can move a mountain. Now I lay no claim to a monumental kind of faith, but I've put all my unborn sons on the altar and slain them (as God asked of Abraham). That, I think without hubris, is a tad larger than a mustard seed. But my soul has a lot of scar tissue on its knuckles from knocking on doors that remained resolutely closed.

One honest way out of this dilemma is, when we feel our prayers go unanswered, that "I'm sorry, but no" is, in fact, an answer. And as we learn definitively from the book of Job, God is not answerable to us. Probably the most profound surrender of our lives is that one: Allowing God to be God, allowing God to have reasons our minds are incapable of comprehending.

But a deeper and better answer, I think, is in the words "taken by itself." Fundamentalists like to do that. If you take turning the other cheek out of the context of Jesus clearing the Temple in a towering rage, Abraham Lincoln and Mohandas Gandhi would be less noble. Just so, you can't honestly grasp the passage about guaranteed prayers unless you couple it with the way Jesus himself prays here in the Garden of Olives: "Let this chalice pass from me, but if it be not your will . . ." And in this case, God's answer is, "I'm sorry, but no." To his own Son.

That one word—"but"—takes from prayer all the elements of magic, all the bargaining and blackmail, all the attempts to manipulate God's will. When Jesus made those promises about fulfilling prayer, that "but" was part of the man saying it, his understanding of God and prayer—just as we, all unwittingly, claim every time we say the Lord's Prayer: "Thy will be done." In the background of these promises, that "but" is a given.

In your imagination, see the Lord's Prayer "in parallel" with the agony in the garden. The prayer is almost a skeletal sketch of the scene.

Truly simpleminded folks say God is a human invention—a placebo so we don't have to face the annihilation of death. That's really dumb. Surely the most uninspired human could come up with a more cooperative, subservient, accommodating God than the one we've got.

Unnerving as that is, it's definitive proof God is in charge and I'm not. I'm glad it is. Because there are a lot of other things I've prayed for that I'm glad I didn't get, and the number of the damned would be significantly larger if my incautious requests were always fulfilled, and life would be a lot duller if God were only as smart—and small-minded—as I am.

The Appointed Time: Kairos—The Cosmic Battle

All Jesus' stories—the landlord coming back unexpectedly, the bridegroom finding the bridesmaids unready, the master finally demanding a tally, the plantation owner sending his agents to the tenant farmers—well, this is it: The landlord has dropped the gauntlet. This *is* the moment: the *kairos*. The ignition of the final cosmic battle between Good and Evil.

Here is one more proof that the Plan is no "plan" at all, some secret we could discern if we only consulted the right shaman or fortune-teller. There are only two fundamental forces. Perhaps Freud denoted them better even than many theologians. He called the two fundamental forces at work within the human soul Eros—the Life Wish—and Thanatos—the Death Wish. Almost the same ungraspable entities we call the Good Spirit and the Evil

Spirit. Eros craves *challenge*, constant rebirth, even at the risk of minideaths: growth, marriage, having children, reaching beyond the usual horizons. Thanatos craves the security of the womb again, being unbothered, unopposed, freed of others' moods and bristles and agendas.

Conflicts between them in everyday life are so often trivial that they take on meaning and genuine opportunity only when we see them with a long-range attitude of Eros or Thanatos.

Just as at the beginning of the book of Job God gave Satan, "the Adversary," free access to "the perfect and upright man," here the Father gives Evil a free hand over his Beloved Son. This is a battle between the Spirit of Light and the Spirit of Darkness. And none of us is exempt.

And the trainees are caught sleeping. Peter, James, and John, privileged to experience whatever the transfiguration entailed, are now present at the beginning of Jesus' degradation. And they pretty much snore through it, as most people today can doze through the Sermon on the Mount. Peter has sworn he would not desert— as he will later swear he never knew this man. But the burden of being human is too wearying. James and John swore they could "drink the cup," and here they pretty much miss Jesus' all-too-human prayer to avoid the terrifying cup himself.

It's reassuring to know they were not always "saints."

Three Lessons

Ron Rolheiser, OMI, offers three insights from sharing with Jesus in the garden: (1) Losing resentment, (2) Accepting humiliation, (3) Sacrificing for the greater good.

Resentment: AA has a wonderful saying, "Resentment is like taking poison and hoping the other guy dies." Just on a human level, nursing grudges is slow soul suicide, and the person who caused our bitterness is none the wiser. But in the garden, Jesus begins his final instruction on how to accept the impossibility of usurping God's place—which was the very first and remains the perennial sin. It's also the theme of every commercial: "Eat this, and you'll become like God!" We'll find "the peace the world cannot give" only when we surrender to the truth that we were created imperfect and asked to deal with an imperfect world.

The healing attitude of Gethsemane is accepting the will of the Father: the challenge to cope with dignity, in an endless thicket of encounters—titanic and trivial—with imperfect family, bosses, government, Church, spouse, body-self. That is the way we possess our souls in a way we can offer them confidently to our neighbors and to God.

Humiliation: Another hint Jesus gives us here is yielding. Washing feet, shucking the urge to superiority, accepting the absurdity of "what I deserve" in a transcosmic perspective, where I did nothing to "deserve" being here in the first place. In a worldview encompassing the degradation of Almighty God, there is no shame in not being quarterback or prom queen. When we finally bow to the easily forgotten truth that Someone Else "has the lead," there's a greater chance we might take joy in merely being in the back of the chorus and not just in the last row in the balcony. The incarnation—and the passion, death, and resurrection—teach us what it's like to be exalted and humbled at the same time. Finding "our place."

Sacrifice for the greater good: In an ethos where the media constantly try to sell couch potatoes torture machines that would have delighted Torquemada, it's laugh making to hear them question the value of foreswearing meat on Lenten Fridays. The same folks who work up almost bloody sweats lifting weights and running marathons bewail the unfairness of the life we find ourselves strapped with. In one area, they understand "purposeful pain," athletic or cosmetic, but can't comprehend why God wasn't smart enough to come up with a world without pain. (They're the same folks who are proabortion but against war and capital punishment.)

Could it be that God does have a purpose in suffering? I'd fight tooth and fang against the explanation that says it's a "test" to see who's worthy of God's love, or of heaven. An all-knowing God has no need of tests. Nor is the all-loving God sadistic.

Another explanation is that suffering is a way God had to resort to in order to "wake us up" to the fact that God is, in fact, God—not answerable to us. Also, as my good friend Bill Fold, dying of cancer, said, "Isn't it wonderful he trusts me enough to give it to me?"

But just as athletic "self-punishment" is a way to make our bodies more resilient, could it be that unmerited suffering hollows our souls in order to hallow them? Life's setbacks wake us from everyday torpor to the God-sized emptiness within each of us that made even the Stones lament, "I can't get no satisfaction"? And Peggy Lee sing, "Is that all there is?" And as Augustine wrote, "Our hearts are restless till they rest in You."

To be too facile: Pain can make a bitter me or better me.

Dr. Martin Luther King, Jr.

About a month before Dr. King was murdered, he singled out one of the many threatening phone calls he received. The caller said, simply, "If you come here we're going to kill you." He'd had life-threatening calls many times before, "But that night, for whatever reason, it shook me to my roots. I couldn't go back to sleep. I brewed some coffee. I drank the whole pot." He said: "I began to cry at the kitchen table, and I lost all my courage." He said: "I put my head in my hands and I thought, I can't do this anymore. I don't want to die."

And he said: "At that moment I felt this strength in me that I had never felt before. I knew what to do, what I needed to do."

There is no resurrection without death. Jesus accepted that. After that agony, we was an athlete who had made his *agonia*. He could walk, head high, to his Passion.

9. The Captive

Yom Shishi: Friday, About 3 A.M.

A ragtag crowd. There were a couple of bored Roman soldiers, loaned reluctantly by the governor for show. Hardly needed at this inconvenient hour of the night. The ones officially delegated were from the Temple—enough sanctuary police to handle a dozen ruffians easily—with the young priestlings safely behind a crowd made up of vagrants, wild boys up too late, and a few curious pilgrims roused from sleep in the valley. And in front, at the point, the apostate, Judas, summoning up his full height. He pulled away from the men with torches and billy clubs and crossed the open space to where Jesus stood in front of his confused and terrified men.

No one could possibly intuit what was going on inside him.

Judas put his hands firmly on Jesus' shoulders and pulled him toward him, kissing him hard on the mouth. "*Master!*" he said, pulling back with a feral grin.

Jesus bowed his head and answered quietly, "My friend." He laid his hand gently on Judas's shoulder and moved him aside. He took a step toward the Temple guard who seemed in charge. "Who have you come out for?"

He was a tired pensioner, ill at ease with this business. "You Jesus? The Nazarene?"

"I am."

The Temple people fell back on one another at the temerity of the words. The young priests blanched at the casual blasphemy.

"I'm the one you're looking for," Jesus said. "Let the others go."

In a blur, Peter pushed past Jesus and ran growling at the intruders with his short sword raised. He swiped wildly with his long knife toward the leader of the guards, but it glanced off his shoulder-guards and hacked the ear of the high priest's slave, a boy carrying his shield.

"I said no *more* of that!" Jesus snapped and crossed to the boy, cowering in shock with his hand to his bloodied ear. Jesus reached up and circled his fingers around the young man's ear, then pulled his hand away. There was no blood left, not even on his fingertips. The lad put his hands to his ear, dumbfounded.

Jesus looked back at his friends. "If that was what we were about, my Father could give me a legion of angels for each one of you. I'm ready. It has to be. Get *behind* me!"

He turned back to the intruders. "And you. Swords and clubs? Am I a hill bandit? Some neighborhood thug? Almost every day I've been right there in the Temple. Teaching. Plenty of witnesses if I'd spoken false."

He reached out his wrists for the ropes. "I'm the one you want. Let them go."

A Temple guard with a coil of rope stepped forward, and his movement triggered a stampede of feet. Every one of Jesus' men fled into the night.

Jesus watched as the darkness absorbed them, and a guard whipped the cord expertly around and between Jesus' wrists.

Then, there was a sudden flash of white behind him. Some young man, wrapped only in a white cloth, pushed past Jesus. The cloth caught against the prisoner's shoulder, fluttered to the hard ground, and the fleeing young man was swallowed up stark naked in the darkness.

Jesus stared after him. "Now," he said. "Now is the dark abyss."

The cloth lay there still. Like a shroud.

Now Jesus was finally bereft. Absolutely alone.

Puzzling Moments

The "Crowd"

This was not a lynch mob of angry vigilantes, as films might suggest. If anything, Jesus was highly respected among whatever ordinary folk even knew he existed and was in the city. Nor did the situation require a significant deployment of armor. These were men hired to police the Temple grounds and keep order there, hardly professionals. As for a priestly presence, no more was needed than a show of their white tunics, hardly the presence of their worthier elders who'd just been rousted from bed to gather officially in the house of Caiphas, the high priest.

The festivals in Jerusalem were always politically volatile, and after the welcome Jesus had received, there was good reason to expect trouble. But the situation here was no more than a dozen men. However, they were all from Galilee, a constant source of ill-trained malcontents, and the nearby wadi was filled with pilgrims from "outside." Still, it was hardly worth more than a token presence from the occupation forces. It does suggest, though, that Pontius Pilate, the Roman governor, was at least obliquely aware Jesus was in the city and a potential problem.

The Kiss of Death

Both Matthew and Mark use the Greek verb *kataphilein*, which means to kiss firmly, intensely, passionately, tenderly or warmly. They both use a more intense word than one that would merely suggest the routine air kisses on both cheeks Middle Eastern men still exchange on a chance meeting. This kiss has a clear *intention*.

The most common interpretation is it was to ensure the guards arrested the right man. But Jesus had made himself more recognizable than one of faceless thousands of out-of-towners. Surely, one or two Temple police would have recalled the face of the outlaw who'd rousted the moneychangers in a chaos of quacking and bellowing. He'd been teaching there daily not just this trip but on previous occasions when the establishment began to take an interest in him.

Judas's main usefulness to the authorities was to lead them to Jesus in a place where his arrest wouldn't cause a disturbance that could ripple out into something serious. It's possible that the arrest was delayed so long after Judas left the supper because he'd taken them first to the upper room, then to the place they had often gone to pray.

This kiss is one of those scriptural occurrences where one says, "If this *didn't* actually happen, it *should* have." It is an act indescribably beyond hypocrisy. Yet it can't have been the cold-blooded caricature of Judas that Dorothy Sayers said was an insult to Jesus' intelligence.

Was this kiss so intense because, like an equally traitorous villain, Macbeth, "I am in blood stepped in so far that, should I wade no more, Returning were as tedious as go o'er." If you choose to lose your soul, do it resolutely. As with all narcissism, the gut need to preserve self-righteousness is more than enough to smother the insupportable truth.

Try to imagine a method actor wrestling to recreate within himself the conflicts in Judas: "What if I'm wrong about him? . . . He has never been anything but kind . . . I did entrust all I held precious in this man . . . he washed my feet. He gave me the cup . . . he's not just another man!"

A more cool-headed approach to the kiss and to all Judas does during the Passion is many allusions back to the Hebrew Scriptures. The patriarch Joseph was sold by one of his eleven brothers for silver; when King David was betrayed by his trusted counselor Ahitophel, David retreated, weeping, to the Mount of Olives, and Ahitophel later hanged himself (2 SAMUEL 17). Also, the minor prophet Zechariah identifies wine with blood of the covenant (9:11), and sets a price on the head of "the shepherd" as thirty pieces of silver hurled into the Temple treasury (11:12-13).

This doesn't impugn the historicity of Judas's suicide nor the other details of the Gospel narratives. It merely reminded the writers of Ahitophel and Zechariah, and they used the allusions to focus this event more meaningfully into the ongoing story of the Really Real.

"I Am"

The Hebrew, *Ehyeh asher ehyeh*, and the Greek, *Ego eimi*, "I AM," are words Yahweh used to identify himself to Moses, the Divine Name, which no pious Jew would enunciate or even write. Today, instructors can tell a student is an observant Jew when he or she writes "G-d" if the word is needed. Other places in the Gospels, the writers resort to circumlocutions like, "As you say" or "You're the one who said that." Or "Lord" (*Kyrios*), "the Most High, the Holy One." In Philippians (2:9-11), Paul says that after Jesus' death:

> God gave him the name
> that is above every name,
> so that at the name of Jesus
> every knee should bend,
> in heaven and on earth and under the earth,
> and every tongue should confess
> that Jesus Christ is Lord.

John has shown Jesus making this claim before, when he said, "Before Abraham was, I am" (8:58). His description here of the "crowd's" reaction indicates Jesus' *intentional* use of that forbidden designation. As Yahweh used the words to designate his nature and role, so does Jesus. Mark will be equally forthright when Caiphas asks Jesus who he is under oath. In fact, "Who is Jesus?" is the theme of Mark's Gospel, climaxing in the Roman centurion's confession that Jesus was, indeed, "the Son of God."

Bandit

The Greek word is *lestes*, a word whose connotations include all sorts of "outlaws" and "brigands." What is worth noting is the crowd before Pilate will cry out for a genuine *lestes*, Barabbas, to be released in his place, and that the two "counselors" crucified with Jesus will be "thieves, outlaws, brigands." Jesus had never been fastidious about his companions.

The Naked Young Man

This enigmatic figure appears only in Mark. This is not mere carelessness; Mark has already said that "*all*" those with Jesus had fled. Who could this puzzling "young man" be?

Was this figure a real person or a symbol of something more meaningful? For years scholars thought it Mark's "signature," that the man was Mark himself, as Hitchcock made a two-second cameo appearance in many of his films. But Mark was quite likely not a Palestinian.

Worthy commentators, including saints John Chrysostom, Ambrose, and Gregory, have suggested this was the equally enigmatic "apostle whom Jesus loved" who appears now several times in the Passion and is often also asserted (with sparse evidence) to be John the apostle, who is also slimly asserted to be the author of the Fourth Gospel. One hyperactive imagination leaps to the conclusion that both the "beloved disciple" and this figure are Jesus' secret male lover. Some say it is merely an OT allusion to virtuous Joseph in Egypt fleeing naked from Potiphar's overeager wife (GENESIS 39), though any parallel there is strained. It has also been suggested that the figure was no more than a pilgrim, tented in the garden somewhere, awakened naked in his bedcover, come to see what all the noise was about. Without a specific name, he can hardly be someone who could be called as an eyewitness. Hardly worth inclusion.

The Greek word translated as "following" is more like "shadowing," dogging Jesus' footsteps. The "white cloth" (*sindon*) was in fact a term used for a shroud. The key to what seems a less strained understanding is that the precise same words, "young man (*neani-skos*)" and "wrapped (*peribeblemenos*)," appear in the New Testament again—*only* in Mark's Gospel: at the resurrection. John has the women at the tomb greeted by two angels, Matthew by one angel, and Luke by two men in brilliant clothes—all consistent OT symbols for angels and/or the presence of God. Only Mark has the women met by "a young man wrapped in a linen cloth," the same two Greek words, rare in the Gospels. Only the word *sindon* is different.

A case could be made, then, that Mark is using this baffling young man to symbolize that Jesus' clear conviction of his relationship with the Father and his mission, which has never faltered since his baptism (concretized here as a naked man in white: angel), now deserts him. His disciples fled; now he loses his previous surety of his mission and of his unfailing divine support. He faces the rest alone, on sheer faith in a silent God.

In her diary Mother Teresa of Calcutta confessed that for the final years of her exemplary Christian life, she, too, felt bereft of that conviction that had sustained her before. "I am told God lives in me—and yet the reality of darkness and coldness and emptiness is so great that nothing touches my soul," she wrote. "I want God with all the power of my soul—and yet between us there is terrible separation. I feel just that terrible pain of loss, of God not wanting me, of God not being God, of God not really existing."

Despite authoritative cavils to the contrary, that understanding of the naked young man "feels" right. Accurate can yield to meaningful.

Elements to Ponder

Dignity

From its opening sentence, the Gospel of John is set on a transcosmic stage, and the Son is a larger-than-life Personage:

In the beginning was the Word, and the Word was with God, and the Word was God. He was in the beginning with God. All things came into being through him, and without him not one thing came into being. What has come into being in him was life, and the life was the light of all people. The light shines in the darkness, and the darkness did not overcome it.

That is the Jesus who emerges strongly in the Fourth Gospel's Passion. This is the Jesus whose radiant, confident spirit causes Pontius Pilate to vacillate, again and again, trying to find some legitimate excuse to dodge the pressure from the priests to execute him. His hesitation was not at condemning an innocent man. He'd done that more than once and felt no compunction. But, as a pagan brought up on stories of gods who interfere in disguise to upset the lives of great men, no matter what his adult skepticism about the otherworldly, Pilate was shrewd enough to sense he had no ordinary man standing battered in front of him.

Like victims of the Nazi camps, no matter what degradations the Enemy can inflict on Jesus' body, they can never defeat his soul.

At the opposite extreme, Jesus in Mark's Passion is utterly bereft, deserted not only by his closest friends, but (if the interpretation here is acceptable, at least for prayerful insight) also denied his sense of the presence and support of his Father. John emphasizes the Son; Mark emphasizes the Man.

This Eternal Word "*became flesh.*" The Greek term for that Eternal Entity is *Logos*. Its connotations are abstract, cool, depersonalized, clinical, erudite—in short, "scientific." In contrast, the Aramaic for that same Entity is *dabhar*, which Diarmuid O'Murchu insists is better translated as "an irresistible creative energy exploding into prodigious creativity." That understanding is closer to fecund primeval swamps than to the cultivated groves of academe. Such insight does not deny rational theology, but it suggests our idea of the Almighty—and our relationship with the

Divinity—is severely impoverished without the corrective of its (seemingly incompatible) opposite.

Caught again on the horns of paradox. But not a contradiction. I offer a corrective to the *exclusively* passive victimhood evoked by Mel Gibson and by medieval piety and so consistent in Passion allusions to Hebrew Scripture: "a worm and no man . . . like a lamb that is led to the slaughter, and like a sheep that before its shearers is silent, so he did not open his mouth."

Like the solid/ethereal electron, like the angel/devil human, the divine/human Jesus was *both* submissive and self-possessed. His life and his soul were not raped from him. He yielded up both—and only when he was good and ready.

Eleanor Roosevelt captured that confidence in humiliation: "No one degrades you without your cooperation." So did that same Isaiah who invoked the sheep metaphor:

> The Lord God helps me;
> therefore I have *not* been disgraced;
> therefore I have set my face like flint,
> and I know that I shall not be put to shame;
> for he who vindicates me is near. (Is 50:7-8,
> my emphasis)

Jesus was victimized. But he was not rendered timid, cowed, sheepish. He relied, wholeheartedly, on the support of his Father. Even when he no longer *felt* it.

God within Us

What could we ordinary Christians find within ourselves enabling us to imitate the God/Man Jesus when we ourselves face challenges—whether a threat to our jobs over a moral choice or even merely the silent sneers of more sophisticated nonbelievers?

Jesus answered the question: "When they bring you to trial and hand you over, do not worry beforehand about what you are to say;

but say whatever is given you at that time, for it is not you who speak, but the Holy Spirit" (Mк 13:11).

We keep running into the same old *mangled* lessons from childhood: "Now don't you go getting *vain!*" The Greek word *hubris* so slovenly translated with the ambivalent word "pride." It did not mean legitimate pride in a job well done. It meant narcissism, arrogance—the self-authentication embodied in Adam and Eve, Oedipus, Nero, Napoleon, Stalin. But as a result of that seemingly trivial semantic choice, centuries of good people have considered themselves "unprofitable servants," mere children to be "seen and not heard." Sheep.

To say "I'm nobody" is, on the one hand, a self-fulfilling prophecy. You act like a nobody and thus will be neither threat nor help to the Kingdom of God. On the other hand, it's *precisely* you nobodies Yahweh has always been on the prowl for since we left Eden: Abram and Sarai, Moses, David, Isaiah, Jeremiah, Mary, Simon Peter.

To belabor the truth once again: unworthiness is the whole *point*! What kind of intelligent God would choose a hillbilly girl as the mother of the Messiah? A charmless cave for the entrance-way of divinity? Twelve lamebrain peasants for the first pope and bishops? A crucified felon as The Ideal of human purpose?

The first lesson any human must learn is: I am not God. But the second lesson is: I am not nobody. The Son of God has offered me adoption. I am not the King. But I have been invited to be a Peer of the Realm. Then *noblesse oblige*. It's time I carried myself as if I actually *believe* what I claim to believe. Perhaps I am not noteworthy, but Jesus Christ has made me meaningful.

10. THE TRIAL OF THE DIVINE MESSIAH

Yom Shishi—Friday—Sometime before Dawn

Some reports claim, after the trek from the garden, across the city, and then into the upper-class neighborhoods, the arresting party turned first into the yard of Annas, the previous high priest, which is possible. The high priest was, effectively, the head of the Jewish nation. Even if Annas was *emeritus*, he remained the power broker, flexible enough to hang on to the office personally for nine years—until he was deposed by the procurator Gratus "for executing capital sentences forbidden by the imperial government." However, his wealth and aristocratic connections still served to keep power in the family as he shepherded his sons and then his son-in-law Caiphas to succeed him twenty years more.

Neither Annas nor Caiphas was shackled to principles resistant to enlightened compromise. A persistent rumor claimed Annas had plans to kill Lazarus, whom Jesus (allegedly) brought back from death, because "on account of him, many Jews were defecting to this Jesus." Also several members of the Sanhedrin, the seventy-two-member High Council, had told not a few others that Caiphas had declared, "If we let this Jesus go on like this, everyone will believe in him, and then the Romans will come and take away both our Temple and our nation. Simple expedience. Let one insignificant man die instead of the whole people!"

When the mob brought Jesus in to Annas, the old man demanded he reveal the names of his disciples and what doctrines he taught. Knowing Annas no longer had genuine authority, Jesus purposely ignored the demand to implicate his followers and said his doctrines were a matter of public knowledge. At that, one of the Temple police back-fisted Jesus across the face. "You think you can talk to the high priest like that?!"

Jesus sucked air through his teeth against the pain and said, "If I said something wrong, tell me what that was. But if I've spoken the truth, why would you want to punish me for that?"

So Annas sent him off, still bound, to Caiphas, the official high priest.

Once Caiphas confirmed with Judas the best time and place to arrest Jesus, he had summoned the Sanhedrin—who, to a man, had a vested interest in the case. He rousted them from sleep in the dead of night and sent agents to round up the witnesses his investigators had already found willing to testify against the accused. No defense witnesses were deemed necessary.

They gathered for a highly unusual night session, not in the customary Chamber of Hewn Stones in the Temple but in the great Hasmonean Palace where the high priest lived, a complex of apartments, offices, courtyards, gardens, and a number of mikvah baths for ritual purification. The long compound was a series of impressive turrets, with its own special guards, barracks, underground prisoner cells, and interrogation chambers. Some of the witnesses waited down there in the cellars to be summoned.

The gate from the street opened into a large courtyard where servants and slaves had been roused to prepare the great banquet hall for the gathering of aristocratic priests and politicians who had drifted in over the last hour or so. Near the gate, some guards and serving girls squatted on the flagstones warming themselves at a fire against the early-morning cold. It was almost summer, with stifling days but numbing nights.

Their chiding banter and jokes hushed when the guards dragged in the prisoner with his hands bound and a rope around his neck like a wayward sheep. His cheeks and lips were bruised and puffy. "It's him . . . Who's him? . . . The Galilean rabble rouser. Just another looney. Or maybe a miracle man. Who's t'tell? You?"

The squad of police dragged the prisoner up the right arm of the curving steps leading to the wide balcony entrance to the central palace. A few hangers-on tried to creep up behind them to listen at the door, but a guard booted them down the steps. When the door had closed into the banquet hall, a few spunky boys crept back up to listen.

The last one to pick himself up at the foot of the stairs was Simon Peter.

A plump serving woman with cheeks like last winter's apple looked up at him as he tried to edge in toward the fire. Her face was tough and wrinkled in the firelight. "Hey, *wait* a minute! I seen *you* with that miracle guy! Maybe a week ago." She looked around at her neighbors. "You remember, dontcha? The big hoo-hah at the Eastern Gate. I was bringin' in my sister and her kids, from Jericho. You saw him, right? The man on a donkey?"

Peter gave her a sour smile. "You're mistaken, woman. I don't even *know* that man. I just saw the fire, and I was cold." He huddled further into his cloak.

On the floor above them, in the huge hall lit with torches and candles, the leaders of the Jews were assembled, the more august members in a row along a carpeted riser where the high table usually sat, while the less important—but still influential—members sat on benches on the floor. The high priest's guards left the prisoner standing alone in the center before Caiphas and withdrew to the far ends of the low platform. The high priest was enthroned in his robes of office: a flowing white gown, a golden scapular with its jeweled breastplate, the puffy mushroom turban.

"Bring in the witnesses," Caiphas ordered.

And so the sad parade began, men obviously shooting eyes to their priestly patrons to be sure they were doing it right. But there was too much of nothing—each testimony damning, but no two alike. "He cured people by magic. I saw it. . . . That last man was wrong. It was the devil. . . . He said him and his men was gonna destroy the Temple . . . no wait! He didn't say he 'was,' he said he 'could.' But I guess it meant the same . . . Alla time, he's with tax collectors. And . . . and whores. He's tarred all over with sins . . . Right! Listen to that man! And this sinner forgave their sins! He said Abraham and Isaac and Jacob wouldn't even reckanize you worthy gentlemen . . . No respect for the Sabbath! None! My brother was a cripple. And this man cured him. And then he told my brother to carry his mat home. On the *Sabbath*! . . . What that other guy said about the Temple. I heard that, too . . . but he wasn't talking about the *real* Temple, fool. There was something in there about 'built by hands.' I remember that! . . . He's *crazy*! He acts like he's so special. Better'n anybody. Better'n *God*!"

One dared to say, "When I was with him he told us we were going to have to eat his *flesh*!" But that charge was so ludicrous they kept calling for others.

The high priest was becoming frustrated. This whole process was taking much too long. If it was to be done right, they still had to persuade the Roman procurator. They couldn't call their best witness, his man Judas. Too clearly tainted. And the whole business had to be out of the way by sundown tonight, before the start of the Sabbath and the holy day.

Meanwhile, down in the courtyard at the fire, a serving man tapped Simon Peter on the arm and said, "That hag was *right*. You *was* with that guy. The one up with the priests. Listen to him. He's talks like a hillbilly. He's a Galilean."

"*Goddammit!*" Peter snapped, bunching his big fists. He jerked to his feet and edged toward the gate. He was huffing and shaking, but not ready to run for it. He heard that same wrinkled nag hollering and pointing at him to the others. Leaning against the hinges of the gate, he bellowed back at them, like a rejected child. "Devil take him! I don't even know that man!"

Caiphas shifted uncomfortably in his great chair. "There's a pattern here," he said, stroking his elegant curly beard. "At the root of what all these men say about you is a question of *power*. We know the wanton havoc you caused in the Temple. The witnesses testified you promised to bring down the sanctuary of our God and of our people. By whatever means. You claim you are greater than all our forefathers! This *authority* you claim. Where does this power come from? Surely, not from *this* divinely constituted body, where the divine power resides. Do you think you have some kind of *divine* power?"

Jesus stood there, trying to stand erect. "If I answer you honestly, you won't believe me. If I question you, you'll refuse to answer. Then neither shall I."

Caiphas grasped the arms of his chair. "Well? Do you realize we have power to take your *life*? Do you have some greater power than we do? Some divine power? *Do* you?"

But Jesus remained silent.

The high priest was beyond exasperated. He thrust himself to his feet and stepped off the platform, leveling his forefinger into Jesus' face: "Hear me, Galilean! I challenge you in the name of the living God! On your *oath*! As you stand before your Maker, *are* you the Messiah? *Are* you the Son of Most High?"

Slowly, Jesus raised his eyes directly into the eyes of the high priest. "I am," he said.

Caiphas couldn't reach deeply enough for a breath.

Jesus kept speaking. "And soon you will see the Son of Man, seated at the right hand of the Great Power, coming on the clouds of heaven!"

The high priest's face was crimson. His hands flew to the neck of his gown and he ripped it halfway down his chest. "From his own *lips*!" he cried.

A clamor of voices spread down the lines of seated priests and elders. Almost as one, they surged to their feet, growling like angry dogs at this man's mad effrontery. Using the name that dare not be spoken? Of *himself*? No decent Jew would abide it. Something ferally holy took hold of them, and they converged on the prisoner like a pack of infuriated jackals. Flailing at him, some of their wild blows falling on one another's heads and shoulders. Aristocrats and reverend men, shouting at a mutant beast. "*Prophesy*, cur! Do you know my name?" In the flurry of long sleeves, their cries were muffled. "Destroy our Temple? . . . Son of Satan! . . . A curse on your blasphemy! . . . He has to be obliterated! . . . Death on him!"

Their judgment was chaotic but incontestable.

As the elders became fatigued and backed off, breathing heavily and grasping the shreds of their dignity, the Temple police moved in to take him down to the cells. The men of the Sanhedrin and the high priest withdrew to purify their hands and rearrange their clothing. They would return for the official sentence at daybreak. Meanwhile, Caiphas sent a messenger to the governor, Pontius Pilate, to warn him that the whole Great Council would attend on his very earliest convenience that morning.

The boys at the top of the stairs hissed, "They're coming out!" and scooted down the two staircases. As the servants moved from the fire back to their work, a man grabbed Peter's sleeve. "You! You were *with* him! On the Mount of Olives. My cousin, Malchus! You cut off his damn ear, you bastard! You're one of his men!"

Peter shrugged off the hand wildly, and shrieked: "*I am . . . not!!!* God strike me down if! . . ." And he kept muttering soldiers' curses at them. He wrenched away just as the guards led Jesus, eyes swollen and nose running blood, down to the cells. Somewhere nearby, a rooster screeched, and Peter's head jerked around, and he stared up the stairway.

He saw the battered Jesus being jostled down, looking over the rail of the staircase, only at him. And he remembered.

Peter's guts clenched like a fist, and he fled out into the night. As he ran he broke into sobs, and he wept. And wept.

Puzzling Questions

Charges/Motives

These reports, we must keep remembering, were compiled by ordinary people waylaying eyewitnesses and begging for any new or corroborative detail. But they were not, unlike today, compiled from sworn statements and carefully recorded court transcripts. At least as far as the four editors were aware, the whole Sanhedrin business was a foregone conclusion. Hostile witnesses only, ready to hand, quite likely suborned—and readied to testify by too many willing conspirators with no coordinated agenda. It seems almost as if this "hearing" is not a trial but rather an investigation trying *to come up with* any kind of sustainable indictment.

If the charges against Jesus are left to educated guess, so too, of course, are the motives behind them.

The real trial—the only one that can be in any sense effective and satisfying—will be the one before Pilate. Lest Jesus become a martyr, he has to die as a civil outlaw. But note that the conclusions of this initiative are exclusively *religious*: Jesus' admission that he is the long-awaited Messiah and that he is equal to God. Therefore, in their time "offstage" here, the major participants have to refocus the charges against the prisoner. The core question remains about *authority* and *power*. The trial that just abruptly concluded was about *their* power, priestly power. Now the question has to be skewed into a charge that would interest Pilate—and in fact even come under his jurisdiction. Not the claim of being the Messiah or even a call on divinity. Rather, a challenge to the power of Caesar: a rebel king.

The Sanctuary

Nothing could provoke the religious sensitivities of observant Jews more fiercely (short of outright insult to the Divinity himself) than perceived affronts to God's preeminent symbol: the Temple of Jerusalem. Recall the later incident of Caligula's statue destined for the Holy of Holies. Thousands of unarmed Jews responded by lying prostrate and offering themselves to Roman soldiers for a mass slaughter. Other Jews threatened an agricultural strike. The governor backed down. In 50 CE, Josephus later reported, a soldier guarding the Temple "raised his robe, stooped in an indecent attitude, so as to turn his backside to the Jews, and made a noise in keeping with his posture." This disrespectful gesture led to a riot and stampede in which (Josephus claimed) over thirty thousand died. When Jesus—purposely, we have to assume—threatened the security and sanctity of the Temple, he was taunting his listeners with a threat non-Jews can hardly appreciate. Perhaps a modern reader might feel similar revulsion hearing threats to violate a child or a nun.

But an awareness of that *sincere* sensitivity within the minds and souls of those who condemned Jesus is essential to avoid the misrepresentation of these religious men as craven mutants, caricatures from *Superstar*, knotting their beards and twisting their rapacious fingers like Fagin or Shylock. Political toadies, intolerant neo-cons. In fairness, we have to accept that doing and saying what Jesus did was like burning a flag outside a construction site. He consorted with society's worst elements, he cavalierly profaned what they held sacred. If the Word became Flesh again, and gave the Sermon on the Mount on TV, every corporate board, every Madison Avenue advertiser, every lobbyist on Earth would be after his head. Like Dostoyevsky's Prince Myshkin or Chayevsky's Howard Beale. There is little profit in prophecy.

But just as Jesus here talks about a conflict on a transcosmic stage much larger than any literal interpretation of the Temple can sustain, in their turn the Hebrew leaders are talking against a background much more concrete and practical than their religious posturing denotes. Probably 20 percent of Jerusalem workers depended on the Temple for their livelihoods; any threat from this up-country hoodlum to destroy that would destroy his popularity. Not to mention that their own opulent lifestyles were completely dependent on the sanctuary's "business."

Even further, like so many politicians, Caiphas couldn't afford to alienate either Pilate or the general public—especially the horde of pilgrims. When all the garbled testimony from the "witnesses" failed to coalesce into any usable charge or sufficient cause for condemnation, this shrewd strategist had to resort to forcing the accused to incriminate himself, under oath.

Blasphemy

There are two charges confused here, too. After twenty centuries of reflection and education, modern Christians hear "Messiah" and "Son of Man" (or "of God") as coterminous, synonymous. To the participants in the present drama, they were not. "Messiah" was pregnant with all the connotations of King David—a royal, military hero. It was presumed the Christ would be a literal linear "Son of David." Thus, when in other versions, Jesus is asked if he is the one expected, and he seems to use equivocations like "You said it," he possibly is saying, "Yes, but not quite the way you intend it." He had already told their spies he was greater than David: "If David thus calls him Lord, how can [the Messiah] be his son?" (Mт 22:45). Jesus soundly rejected any notion of a messiah shielded from suffering and death, with the trappings of royal or military power, or who used family connections.

On the other hand, Jesus' acceptance of "Son of God (the Most High)" cannot be merely a commonly accepted understanding of the term as "a decent man," a worthy person of whom God would approve. The Sanhedrin's dramatic response clearly negates that understanding. If anyone wants to waffle the term, it was certainly what Jesus' hearers *heard*. What he *intended* them to hear. Moreover, it was what the Gospel writers intended their audiences to hear and, under testimony of their martyrdoms, what those audiences did in fact understand.

Nor should there be apprehension about the fact that the other evangelists seem to "come up short" of Mark's relentlessly forthright response of Jesus: "I am!!" (*Ego eimi*), the equivalent of God's self-identification to Moses. Matthew words his response as "*You* have said it" and Luke puts it: "*You* say that I am." Each of those could be read as neutral or noncommittal, as in "Your words, not mine."

Whether Jesus actually said "I am" and *meant* it as God's name, and whether the judges heard him claiming something *that* extreme, he was clearly condemned for *blasphemy*. There is no insult to God—only sheer arrogance—in claiming to be the Messiah if he was not. There would be serious sanction for being a "false prophet," leading the people astray. And Jesus did compare himself to prophets (Mk 6:4; Mt 23:37; Jn 13:33). That would justify condemnation, even to death, but not the violence of the judges' instinctive response.

Nor would Jesus *necessarily* be condemned for making himself God, which would rather suggest he was a madman. But there is no doubt Jesus clear-headedly claimed for himself what belongs only to God and thus, if unfounded, was outright blasphemy. He claimed, even in this trial, that he fulfilled the description of the glorious *Son of Man* in Daniel's prophecy:

Behold, with the clouds of heaven

there came one like a Son of Man,
and he came to the Ancient of Days
　and was presented before him.
And to him was given dominion
　and glory and a kingdom,
that all peoples, nations, and languages
　should serve him;
his dominion is an everlasting dominion,
　which shall not pass away,
and his kingdom one
　that shall not be destroyed. (7:13-14)

This is a celestial exaltation Jesus unarguably assigned to himself. Equivalently, he is saying, "You judge me now, but—at the very end—I will be judging you." Try to hear that with *these* men's ears. Uncountable times, he claimed exclusively divine power to forgive sin. He was repeatedly admonished by officials for flouting accepted standards of holiness. In the present day, think of the Christian-in-the-street's skepticism of faith healers, or of "old Catholics" monitoring religious performances and reporting them in outrage to diocesan offices.

Conclusively, asked under oath if he did indeed claim to be the very God, he affirmed the charge! On the ground of that response, his accusers concluded that he *deserved* to die. He was mocked, battered, and dragged off to a dungeon to await daybreak, when the verdict would be "validated" and the sentence brought to the only authority who could execute.

Anyone who makes the vacuous assertion, "Well, Jesus was a nice moral teacher, but . . ." has a shallower understanding of him than those who murdered him.

These men who condemned Jesus did not seek his death because Jesus merely wanted us to avoid hurting others or breaking justified laws. You don't execute an irrelevance. They wanted him killed because he claimed equality with God. And he refused to shut up about it.

Clerical Mockery and Abuse

Luke, the gentlest evangelist, seemed to have found it impossible to picture the Savior, his hands tied, so villainously attacked by these august personages. Instead, he places the abuse at the hands of "those who held him." However, the Law required that a blasphemer's judges be the first to punish him. On the other hand, the same Law required that judges condemning any criminal to death should mourn and fast all day before ratifying the most irreversible sentence. The Scriptures, at least, make no note of their observing that law in this case.

That moment in the scene is heightened by the worshipful judges, in a grotesque version of the centuries-old game "Blind Man's Bluff," taunting their victim to prophesy who struck him. Prophecy was a test of the authentic Messiah to which this candidate refused to rise.

Illegalities

It is clear that adherence to the written Law was of intense importance to the Hebrews. They boasted scrupulously researched and defined canons of jurisprudence. The Law was their lifeline to God. But in this case, they were tragically like the Nazis in regard to later Jews. Hitler would not make an immoral move unless he had previously forged a law to "justify" it.

Shelves of volumes have been written solely on the manifest infractions of Jewish Law evident in this most significant trial in human history. There is no need to bewilder the reader with any more than the most obvious improprieties. First, the most refined conclusions of modern legal experts about this first-century Jewish trial are like the efforts of modern doctors to draw literal medical conclusions from reportage not only heavily enhanced by theological/ literary/apologetic convictions but that is also based on flimsy documentation and on the same sort of fragile evidence we have about the trials of Socrates and Catiline. Nor were first-century aristocrats as concerned with legal procedure as later rabbis were when they codified the Mishnah, the oral Torah finalized in written documents, nearly a hundred years after this trial.

Moreover, modern volumes—carefully researched and professionally critiqued—are often primarily concerned to lessen the crass treatment of Jesus by "the Jews," which has given rise to virulent anti-Semitism for two millennia. But it is beyond denial that the movement to crucify the founder of Christianity arose among Jews and not from any Roman animus. Furthermore, judging from reports about the aristocratic (mostly Sadducee) Temple priests from their enemies, like Pharisees and Essenes, the injustice of these priests is hardly surprising in this individual case of Jesus. Power corrupts. Coercive authority and dogmatic certitude are lethal in the hands of those who operate on the principle of enlightened self-interest. Just from what we know of the behavior of *any* society's leaders, we can't restrict a judgment of corruption only to this six-dozen first-century Jews. This is but one in tens of thousands of cases of corruptive power.

Yet another reason for caution in assessing—then passing judgment on—the particulars of this trial is that none of the four evangelists was unbiased when it came to the Jewish hierarchy. Matthew and Mark, with good reason—or at least with understandable human resentment—felt a virulent antagonism against the Sanhedrin, whose successors were viciously prosecuting Christian converts in Palestine and Rome at the very time those two were editing their books.

Nonetheless, the improprieties, even allowing for exaggerations, are manifold. In the first place, a capital-case night trial was illegal, which is why Luke has "another" meeting in the morning to give it some spurious justification.

At least according to the only reports we have, Judas—the prime witness—was bribed but never called to testify. Neither were any defense witnesses. The charges are never focused in the trial until *after* the witnesses had proven unsatisfactory. In any society we know, self-incrimination is unjust and forbidden. And the defendant's response in this "trial" is not admission to an accusation, but his response *is the crime in itself.*

We can be certain of few specifics. What is incontestable is that Jesus of Nazareth was condemned by the leaders of his own nation and religion for claiming equality with God.

Beyond that, the only question is whether he was telling the truth. Or was a liar. Or insane.

Elements to Ponder

Enlightened Self-Interest

In the modern electronic matrix where ethical ideals are neutralized by the capitalist profit motive and the need for reassuring consensus, it is sometimes a task worthy of Diogenes to find someone truly principled. On the wider stage, any action seems validated merely by an assertion that this is necessary "for national security" or "for the good of the whole Church."

However, fifty years of teaching in high schools and universities has convinced me that our schooling, even in religious institutions, has had scant effect on the acquisitiveness we inherited from our simian ancestors and is reinforced by every commercial. Self-deception is by no means limited to the arrogant world-beaters. "I'm an honest person. I cheat *only* if I have need and opportunity." Or, "You hear it all the time on cop shows and on courtroom television: 'Innocent until *proven* guilty.'"

It could be a worthy self-examination to scribble out a list of the petty narcissisms one finds so habitual they seem justified by "Well, that's just the way I *am*." Procrastination treated as if it were some kind of inherited disease. (It is, of course. Inherited not necessarily from Adam and Eve, but inescapably from King Kong and Cheetah.) Spitting gum into a drinking fountain.

Parking in a handicapped space. Leaving the toilet roll empty. And what else?

Peter

In trying to understand what really goes on in a Gospel passage, or in trying to use the Ignatian method of prayer which "infuses" oneself into the scene with the other characters of the Gospels, I've previously suggested we imagine an actor trying to prepare to play a particular role and understand a scene from that character's point of view. Any actor would be hard pressed if given the choice to play either Peter or Judas. But once the choice is made, either the actor or the one praying has to strive mightily against the temptation to inhabit a caricature. In getting into the first pope's skin, the too-easy choice is between two oversimplifications: Peter, the bumbling blowhard, and Judas, the conniving snake. Not just too easy but grossly unfair to both. Keep in mind each was purposefully chosen by the most insightful judge of human hearts who ever lived. Jesus found in each of these men something to love, profoundly.

Here we have the rambunctious Peter who stepped fearlessly (at first) out onto the stormy waves. But that same Peter "came to his senses" and asked himself, "What in hell am I trying to do out here?" He's the Peter who, out of all of them, declared bluntly, "You're the Christ! To whom else shall we go?" He's the Peter who at his peril *did* "follow him—at a distance."

The paradox is strong. At the very moment Jesus, under oath, admitted who he really was, his chosen successor was denying—with many oaths—that he even knew the man.

This same Peter was the second Christian apostate, after Judas. He denied Christ, with ferocious soldiers' oaths. Not to a soldier, but to a waitress. And within hours of his ordination, his first Mass, and his first Communion. And yet, after all that, Christ made him the first pope.

The Temple Officials

Some highly respected Christians—Augustine, Chrysostom, Aquinas, Luther—disparaged Jews with a most unchristian ferocity. Until 1960, all Catholics prayed in the Lenten *Improperia* for "the perfidious Jews." Pius XII began the shift, and Vatican II closed the question.

Tsunamis of ink have been poured out trying to absolve the whole Jewish nation—and all their progeny unto the Final Trumpet—from the accusation of being "Christ killers." In the process there has to be a great deal of learned tap-dancing to clear the evangelists from an angry prejudice they quite likely really *did* feel and could hardly exorcize from their writing.

Rather than waste so much well-intentioned effort whitewashing a brindled bull, wouldn't it be less effort—and more honest—to admit that the common Jew-in-the-street had no power whatever, either religious or civil, and made not the slightest meaningful contribution to the decision to kill Jesus? Any shouts they may have hurled at Pilate about accepting the guilt on themselves and their children was generated by paid cheerleaders seeded among them, if those cries are in fact historical at all, and not the editorial bias of the writers. Even actual Jews on the spot, much less their centuries-distant offspring, were no more guilty of deicide than the people of Munich, then or today, were responsible for Hitler's beer hall putsch in 1923 or today's Japanese are culpable for Pearl Harbor.

Can we all acknowledge that, like every human since Eden, those who did condemn Christ were human beings, no more nor less prone to self-protectiveness than we ourselves? They were a tantalizing mixture of insincerity, cunning, fanaticism, and power-hunger.

But we are also left with the universal need in each human being to be the sterling hero or heroine of their own stories. Forget the unjust blame of the ordinary Jew for Christ's death. No matter what obloquy has fallen on their heads, most of the men who did vote to execute Jesus believed—given their lifetime, bone-rooted convictions—they were doing the *right thing*. They were not innocent. What they were guilty of was holding impregnable certitudes, not deicide.

Just as some of us feel resentment for being accused of an original sin committed by two numbhead nudists in Eden, long before there were clocks or laws, so any Jew today has a right to be angry at being accused of the judicial murder of a Galilean rabbi twenty centuries ago.

11. The Trial of the Rebel King

Yom Shishi (Friday)—Around Dawn

By daybreak, time had become more pressing for the priests. He had to be dead by sundown. Or else hang there like a challenge for another full day. Someone had to research the Law on crucified felons still alive on the Sabbath. Not to mention Passover.

In the Hasmonean hall, Caiphas had just secured a nearly unanimous vote that the charge to Pilate would be "perverting our nation and forbidding the common folk to pay civil taxes." Neither of which had to be parsed too cautiously. On internal matters, the present procurator was happy to sign off on whatever trivial parochial matter they assured him was well grounded. It was a mutually satisfying result of their bilateral contempt for one another. The decisive factor was: "Setting himself up as the Messiah, a king in defiance of Caesar." The one or two who suggested that death might be too extreme were hollered to silence.

No sooner was the verdict ratified than the outside door flew open, and Judas stood there on the platform above the courtyard. Someone had been listening and spread the verdict. A guard moved to apprehend him, but the high priest held up his hand. They needed no delays.

"You said nothing about *killing* him!" Judas shouted.

"What business is that of yours, Galilean!" Caiphas asked.

"I've sinned! I've betrayed innocent blood!"

"And what business is that of *ours*!" Caiphas snapped.

Judas hurled the bag of silver at the high priest, and it spilled open at his feet, coins glittering. Judas fled out the door, down the stairs, and out into the streets, raging to himself.

Caiphas bent and pinched the end of his sleeve on the bag and lifted it like a dead rodent, handing it off to a guard. "If that madman believes this is blood money—who knows where he got that absurd notion—we can't let it pollute the treasury. Do I hear a motion? Quickly now!"

After very little time the assembly yielded to the suggestion of one ancient priest who said one of the prophets—Jeremiah or Zechariah, he was unsure at the moment—spoke of thirty silver shekels buying the Field of Blood to bury indigents and criminals, the potter's field where the blood from sacrifices sluiced out below the Temple into the Hinnom ravine. Only a few in the chamber understood why the old priest had hit upon the number thirty.

That matter expeditiously dealt with, the Hebrew leaders summoned the convict from the cellars, gathered themselves and their belongings and headed as a large group toward the praetorium, where they were assured the governor would (reluctantly) begin court earlier than usual to accede to their unpredictable needs.

Word later got round that Judas had hanged himself.

The street and courtyard outside the Roman praetorium was dominated by a wide balcony at the center of which was a square granite throne on which the governor sat to finalize a judgment. Caiphas and one or two experts in Jewish and Roman law waited on the platform above, unused to either subservience or waiting. If Pilate were to deal with them, he was forced to come out to them lest, by entering his chambers, they be defiled and unable to celebrate the feast. The prisoner stood humbly between them and the doorway. The other priests gathered below the steps to the rostrum. As the morning wore on, the indolent and curious began to gather around them. Prepared for such an eventuality, the religious officials had planted hirelings among them like a Greek chorus to assure a proper response to any issue requiring reinforcement and intimidation.

The man they awaited was Pontius Pilate, a longtime soldier with influential connections. In the six years of his prefecture, he'd been admonished more than once for lack of tact regarding the religious sensibilities and practices of the obstinately oversensitive Jews. For instance, he had brazenly sent his soldiers into the city with the loathsome images of the so-called divine Emperor dangling from their unit standards. He had a justified reputation for being headstrong, strict, brusque, and eruptive, and yet like all opportunists, he was both rational and practical. His two principal mandates were collecting taxes and keeping the peace. For lesser issues, just as every commander anywhere and every other governor in the empire, he handled the Jews in whatever ways he deemed necessary on the spot. Perhaps one reason he and Caiphas detested one another so thoroughly was their similarity beneath the cultural disparities.

Quite likely, the governor delayed an entrance to this earlier than usual starting time in order to make clear where the true power lay in any possible conflict.

When he finally made an appearance, guards took their places on both sides of the entrance. He was clad in a white tunic, swathed in a white toga edged with a maroon stripe. Pilate waited until the priests offered him the very slightest of deferential head-bows.

When they spoke, both governor and priests spoke in trained "public voices" for the crowd. Although the people down in the street were unlettered nobodies, little better than useful animals, their ignorant convictions could be lethal when combined with their accumulated force to disrupt the peace.

"What charge?" Pilate asked, tersely.

Caiphas smiled sourly. "If we had not established unquestionably that he was a criminal, we would not have brought him to you . . . sir."

Pilate, knowing their game, snorted, "Fine. Then take him yourselves and punish him as your Law dictates."

But Caiphas answered, pursing his lips, "We are . . . no longer . . . permitted to execute."

"Death?" Pilate asked. "And what can this man have done to deserve execution? I've heard rumors about him. He only wants people to be honest. Why crucify a bleeding-heart?"

One of the lawyers edged to the side of the high priest. "Perverting the people's values, forbidding imperial taxes, promoting himself as the Messiah—a *king* in defiance of the Emperor."

Pilate snapped his fingers at the guard and nodded at the door. The soldier leaped to open it and the procurator entered, the soldier taking the prisoner's elbow and ushering him inside. The hierarchs scowled at being left standing.

In the inner chamber, Pilate turned and squared himself before the prisoner, arms akimbo. "Well?" he snapped. "*Are* you the King of the Jews?"

Jesus raised his battered face. "Those are the words they chose. Are you asking sincerely or merely because they told you I claimed it?"

Pilate huffed. "Am I a Jew? Every climber in this city wants me to crucify you. What've you done to set them off?"

"My kingdom is not a this-world kingdom. If it were, my followers would never have let me be handed over to those men."

Pilate crossed his arms. "So. You *are* some kind of king, then."

"Not as you use the word. I came into the world to testify to the truth."

Pilate snickered. "Truth? That's a laugh. What *is* truth?" He marveled at the man's naivete. "You hear what these men accuse you of? *Are* you a rebel? *Do* you defy the Emperor?"

But Jesus was silent. The rough-hewn governor scowled. Perplexed. But he was aware of the edginess of the priests, which pleased him. He was also hearing the unrest of the growing crowd. Wasn't this the rube they made such a fuss over last weekend? When all the wogs called him "the king"? He began to get the infuriating sense that he was the one they were putting on trial. What happened meanwhile to change their minds? This fool must have done something.

He turned and headed for the door, gesturing for the guard to bring the prisoner. The man was either a saint or a simpleton.

The crowd was swelling now the news had gotten out that he'd been condemned to death for blasphemy and the mucky-mucks were trying to lay the judgment off on this pagan. Most were their own bosses. Worth an hour off work to watch the show.

Pilate spoke over the balustrade to the crowd rather than to the Temple dignitaries. "I find no cause in this prisoner! Therefore, I will have him flogged as a warning and release him."

But by now many realized he'd betrayed their expectations of a Liberator—simply by being stopped. And they'd heard he'd claimed to be equal to God. A madman. Or a charlatan. Thumbs down to him, then. They set up a roar that was unintelligible but still an angry warning. The only reason Pilate had come to town from the delightful seacoast was to clamp down on just such a situation. He had no appetite for these trivialities, but it was best to snuff the spark.

The governor batted his hands for them to quiet down. He could see the only reason the priests had brought this empty-headed fellow was that he might be a threat to their influence. But this time they were playing against a professional. "All right!" he shouted. "I can find no case against this quack that makes him a threat to public order. There is no reason to condemn him. But you have a custom that at the feast the governor grants clemency to one prisoner of the people's choosing. As a gesture of good will, I will release this . . ."

"*No!*" shouted a single trained voice from the now restive crowd. "*Barabbas!*"

And gradually all the fools took up the chant: "Barabbas! Barabbas! Barrabas!"

Barabbas was a notorious prisoner bound over with a bunch of murderous rioters. The blackguard was a kind of folk hero to the witless mob who were always looking for some arrogant boaster to sneer from behind. Many sheep learn how to roar inside a mob.

"I'll release your 'King of the Jews.' That's what your leaders call him."

But the Temple agents had been scooting among the crowd whispering, "Last night! With the priests! He says he *is* God!" The last flicker of their hope sputtered out that he was the One. What decent Jew could argue for him? Maybe not death, but surely he had to be silenced. To claim equality with the Most High was worse than murder.

They began to seethe like a herd possessed by demons. "Barabbas! Barabbas!"

Just at that moment, as the governor strode to the judgment seat to finalize this tedious charade, a guard appeared at the doorway with a wax tablet in hand. Any other time, Pilate would have torn his head off for the intrusion, unless the Emperor had died or the Britons were invading. Now, he was glad for the excuse. He snatched the tablet. A message from his wife, Procula. Since she had arrived in the country, she'd been constantly exasperated by these closed-minded priests, and her note simply warned him to have nothing to do with this innocent man. She had had a dream. Of all the . . . But he put his forehead into his hand as if it were a matter of far greater moment. Then he rose and again raised his hands to quiet the cries for Barabbas.

"Wait! I will put this into the hands of Fate," he cried. "I will scourge a confession from him." Without another word, he turned in to the inner chambers, leaving the worthy priests and the unwashed mob to cool their heels while their King was put to the test.

The soldiers grabbed the prisoner and took him inside, then down to an inner courtyard. Flagellation was always the preliminary to crucifixion. It rendered the condemned less troublesome, like softening up a bull for the kill. The results might also be enough to satisfy this mad mob's bloodlust and thwart the imperious priests.

As Pilate returned to the balustrade, he ostentatiously signaled a guard to bring him a basin and ewer of water from the inner chamber. When it was brought, he dipped his hands ceremoniously into the basin, shook off the water, and reached for the towel. "I wash my hands of this man's blood," he shouted to the crowd. "The responsibility is yours."

He went back into the praesidium to wait as this tiresome business dragged on.

Light was beginning to bleed over the roof into the inner courtyard of the praetorium. In the center, chains dangled from a headless pillar, and the soldiers quickly manacled the prisoner and stripped him naked except for his loin cloth. Nakedness was unfitting for a king!

Six men picked up their equipment, whips with seven braided leather straps, studded randomly with lead rivets and sharp bones. It was a disgusting job, so it usually fell to husky barbarians from around the empire condemned to hard army labor. The limit was forty strokes, but they would stop at thirty-nine, to be safe. Not because of a law but lest the prisoner elude execution.

Two at a time, the chastisers whirled the whips overhead, ran full tilt toward the stone pillar, and released the lash. The whips whistled and struck flesh. At first, the prisoner's skin merely shivered, then it bruised. He began to grunt at each pass, like a dumb ox. But as each pair of executioners yielded to the next, the scourges dug more deeply into the flesh. The whips curled around the belly and buttocks and licked around the legs. Blood began to ooze, then as the rawhide cut into muscle, blood flowed freely, all over the prisoner's body.

As each pair moved back, the *decurio* of the squad shouted, "Tell us, Jew! *Are* you the king? Should Caesar start crapping his pants, Great One! Tell us . . ." And on and on. The prisoner fell to his knees twice, but resolutely, stupidly, struggled back to his feet again.

It took little more than a quarter-hour. No worthwhile result, except for the gore.

They had orders from the top to drag it out, so during the scourging one clever lad took a pliers and braided a circlet of the spiky thornbush tinder near the fire. It looked just like a crown. When the whip men s finished and were wiping off the sweat, a couple of soldiers threw the prisoner's own tunic back over his head and pulled it down over his sodden loincloth. Shock had released his urine. Cloth stuck in the blood, and it was soon splotched red. They stumbled him to a stool near the fire, and one draped one of their scarlet cloaks on his shoulders. "Against the cold, my noble lord," even though the sun was up and they'd all begun to sweat.

The cunning boy with the thorn circlet set it gingerly on the prisoner's head, and the *decurio* found it so right he giggled and hammered it down with his billy club and, with a clumsy flourish, bestowed the club into the prisoner's stiff fist. "Your scepter, Your Royal Dunghood!"

The soldiers fell to their knees, wailing their adoration. "Oh, divine majesty! . . . Oh, hail, King of the Jews! . . . How handsome you look, my noble lord! . . . Make me a citizen, King?"

Word came down from upstairs that it had gone on long enough. So they took him back up to the public portico.

Pilate had seen worse, but the result was good enough to shock the brainless mob. He pushed the savaged prisoner to the railing.

"There he is," the governor cried out to them. "Your *King!*" He turned him slowly round, like a grotesque in an anatomy class.

But all the mob could shout was "Crucify him! Crucify him!"

"Crucify your *King?*" Pilate shouted.

And the chorus came back: "We have no king but Caesar!" Even from the priests.

Caiphas and the lawyers stumbled over one another trying to make him listen. "We have a *Law!* . . . The Law says he *must* die! . . . He must die! . . . He claimed that he's *God!*"

Pilate jerked his head to them. "God? He says he's a *god?*"

"*Ye-e-es!*" the three officials shouted back at him.

Pilate turned back into his chambers, jerking his head at the guards. They took the prisoner's arms, and he nearly went to his knees, but he stiffened and shuffled through the door.

"I have no truck with gods anymore," Pilate snapped. "Oh, we used to have gods aplenty! We'll have none of that! No evil eyes or curses on my children, do you hear? Tell me that you are *not* a god! Do you want to die? Do you realize I can let you *go?* If you give me some slightest bit of humility to outwit those jackals, damn you! I can *outpower* them!"

Jesus twisted his battered jaw and said, "You have . . . power to . . . but not . . . the right to. You would have . . . no power . . . unless it came . . . from above. Those who . . . handed me to . . . are worse."

The governor lost all patience and whisked back out onto the balcony, the prisoner dragged along behind him. Pilate opened his mouth to speak, but Caiphas overrode him with a harsh whisper.

"If you release him, word will certainly get to Caesar that you released a rebel king."

Without turning, Pilate shouted to the crowd, "Shall I crucify your king?"

And the voices thundered back, "Crucify him! Crucify him! Crucify him!"

Pilate looked at the three priests as if they were clods of carrion. "Take him," he said, bypassing the judgment seat and turning into the praesidium.

It hadn't been a total loss. He made them admit they'd given the emperor their souls.

The business had dragged on for the whole morning. It was about noon. The enormous Temple courtyards had already begun to fill with sellers and livestock, with worshipers from all over the world. Thousands and thousands of animals were lining up to have their throats cut. Their bellowing and groans and screeches began to rise over the great walls.

As the Passover animals groaned to the slaughter, the King was herded into the streets.

Puzzling Moments

Pilate

This governor is as fascinating and multifaceted a character as Peter and Judas. And because of our Nicene Creed, his name is more often spoken by Christians than the names of most saints or that of any Caesar. But he was truly not a ready candidate for conversion—even to basic humanity.

The vacillating man pictured in all four Gospels is a sharp contrast to what we know from any other nonscriptural source, which is what makes him interesting. Quite likely, Jesus' calm confidence before torture and imminent, disgraceful death would impress a hard-boiled veteran of battle and political infighting. Just as a man, Jesus was baffling. But efforts at softening the inflexible, self-centered politician we grasp from other professional historians of the time—by appealing to a sudden and quite contradictory squeeze of conscience in the presence of this otherworldly carpenter—are diverting but as unlikely as a Jew giving a heartfelt "Heil Hitler!"

Power is precious to officials with narrow perspectives. To his credit, Pilate takes all other charges no more seriously than Jesus does. They both know how specious they are and motivated by parochial self-protectiveness. But even though Pilate's frame of reference for judgments is broader than that of the insular Jewish priests, it still remains limited to the extent of the Roman Empire. No matter how extensive that was in terms of geography, wealth, or coercive power, it paled equally in the face of the perspective in which Jesus passed judgments.

A more persuasive motive for Pilate's delaying tactics, I believe, is the antagonism of small minds about personal power, which is clearly a theme of the entire Gospel message. Like every Roman, Pilate held every non-Roman in utter disdain. And they returned the favor. We have seen, rightly, this event as the penultimate conflict in a battle between Good and Evil, light and darkness. It is that. But anyone used to the Divinity's consistent appetite for irony and paradox has to see that, as is usual in our everyday lives, that transcosmic struggle is most often reduced to pettiness. In this case, a two-bit politician fighting a back-alley fist fight with a pack of religious bureaucrats over the claims of an omnipotent God who is willing to die for their freedom from death.

A case might be made that such pettiness at the root of widespread human agony is not yet exorcized even from Christian souls. Vietnam War metaphors involving "end runs," "game plans," and "penetrating the enemy's end zone" suggest the same small-mindedness. The same could be said of war movies and video games children play, routinely vaporizing humanoids.

Perhaps the same might be said of those in the crowd scenes at this trial and the soldiers' sadistic treatment of this hillbilly messiah. No need to research mid-Eastern children's games of mockery in the first century. Merely look out the back window of any grade school on Earth and watch the treatment of nonathletic little boys and overweight little girls. Or at a "higher" level skinheads circling a black or a gay man. Like those who served as guards in concentration camps, those crowded below Pilate's balcony, or the soldiers at his behest, were probably "generally good people," unlikely even to kick their neighbor's screeching cat. Little need to strain for a surge of conscience or justice in Pilate. He was born a man.

Herod

Luke (and only Luke) shows Pilate using the priests' mention of Jesus' origin in Galilee and sending him off to the puppet king of that area. Likely more to avoid yielding to these arrogant priests than any altruistic motive of doing justice. It serves several editorial purposes: It irritates the priests, which delights Pilate. It is a way for Pilate to fob off a decision favoring them in this trivial case—or at least drag it out. And if Herod agrees to the sentence, one of their own did their bidding, not the Romans. But also, for Luke, it adds another prominent figure who abjures responsibility for the death of the Messiah.

I omitted it for two reasons: First, just as Pilate hoped, it drags out the suspense, but more importantly history shows that one of the few characterizations *Superstar* got right was the barbarically hedonistic portrayal of the Galilean King. Luke pictures Herod's delight at having a chance to see Jesus do a miracle ("walk across my swimming pool"). Second, I couldn't imagine this self-indulgent decadent getting up at six in the morning. For anything.

Barabbas

He was likely awaiting final sentence until Pilate's arrival from the coast. The word is *lestes*, a catchall for "highwayman, robber, thief, petty rebel." Interestingly, the same word (*lestai*) is used for the two criminals crucified with Jesus. None of the writers suggests they were in the same bloody ruckus as Barabbas. Their names are not quoted in the Gospels and yet the name of "Barabbas," a petty criminal, is explicit. It suggests Barabbas was a ringleader, and the crowd's preference could be attributed not just to their receptivity to the cheerleaders but a kind of obstinate affection for a Robin Hood.

But "Barabbas" is also a patronymic, that is, "son of a man named 'Abbas.'" Some suggest his personal name was also "Jeshua," like Jesus, and his father's name was recalled to separate him from Jesus Bar-Joseph. More importantly, even if a criminal named Barabbas never existed, or was never involved in this trial, the editorial use of him *works*.

First, the name means, literally, "Son of the Father." Which is what Jesus has claimed himself to be all along. And the irony is delicious: the "people" choose to release a man with that name who is—judicially—already condemned for the very crime of which Jesus is wrongly accused. Once again, *if* it didn't really happen, it *should* have.

Blood Guilt

The attentive reader might have noticed I chose to omit Matthew's ruthlessly forthright inclusion of "His blood be on us and on our children" (27:25) from "the people" (*ho laos*). First, it has become as repugnant as "the N word," a battle cry for arrogant ignorance for two thousand years. Second, it's problematic with what intensity Matthew *wanted* his audience to receive it—which is the touchstone of all scriptural understanding. Probably a Jew himself and possibly a former legal scholar, with a rabbinical style, he and his audience were beleaguered and threatened with physical punishment and death for their apostasy from official Judaism. Quite likely, he wrote after the literal destruction of the Temple and is offering a broader reason for its ruin. But third, it seemed needless to belabor what was thoroughly obvious from all the other evidence: The evangelists restricted radical blame for the death of Jesus only to "the Jews"—whatever individuals or groups they intended that to include.

Judas is exonerated at least by his repentance in returning the "blood money." Pilate—the symbol of Roman and civil power—washed his hands of responsibility. (In fact, his Roman wife is the only person, in any source, at any time, who stands up for Jesus.) The unthinking common people in the mob were manipulated; the soldiers were merely exhibiting the savagery humans inherited from apes or from Adam, which civilization tries to domesticate. To them, Jesus was no more a "martyr" than a modern missionary killed for no religious reason but merely for money or sport. Or obedience.

Although the priests sought Jesus' life at the price of a bribe, they hoped they would be unsullied by the coins themselves.

Matthew's instinct—like Mel Gilson's—is for dramatic Grand Guignol. He has a taste for pyrotechnics, like the bodies disentombed at Jesus' death. He uses dreams (Pilate's wife, the Gentile Magi, Joseph [three times]). Like many disillusioned converts—even atheists disenchanted with formal religion—Matthew is sharply critical of his past illusions.

The feeling of blood guilt is echoed in Luke's Acts (5:27-30) when Peter and others were hauled into the Temple:

> And when they had brought them, they set them before the council. And the high priest questioned them, saying, "We strictly charged you not to teach in this name, yet here you have filled Jerusalem with your teaching and you intend to bring this man's blood upon us." But Peter and the apostles answered, "We must obey God rather than men. The God of our fathers raised Jesus whom you killed by hanging him on a tree."

No one can evade the suspicion that Matthew intended to lay the blame for the death of Jesus squarely on the establishment—but also—at least obliquely—on the whole nation.

Whether God holds such a grudge is hard to imagine, but in any case that judgment is up to God, not us.

He Was *Guilty*

Jesus never claimed, flat out, "I am God." Had he done that, he would have been deserted on the spot by fiercely monotheistic Jews. But the Gospels had established long before the Passion that Jesus had at least *claimed* powers and prerogatives restricted only to God. Just what that might mean engaged the minds of churchmen for centuries more, caused schisms, the Reformation, and, at least tangentially, the Enlightenment. It is unjust to critique the "blindness" of seventy-two first-century men of the Sanhedrin for lacking knowledge of twenty centuries of study—all of which still remains inadequate to its "Subject."

Mark's first sentence claims: "This is the good news of Jesus Christ, the Son of God." Matthew's first chapter: "They shall call him Emmanuel, which means 'God is with us'" (1:23). As early as the infancy narratives, Luke (2:14) shows the shepherds hearing an angel (the presence of God) testify that the child they will find is "the Messiah, the Lord [*kyrios*]." John's opening is an operatic confession of the transcosmic hero of his book, and throughout Jesus makes grandiose claims—unless they are true: "[The Father] has given all judgment to the Son, so that all may honor the Son just as they honor the Father" (5:22-23); "Can you say that one whom the Father has sanctified and sent into the world is blaspheming because I said, 'I am God's Son'?" (Jn 10:36); "I and the Father are one" (Jn 10:30); "Before Abraham was, I am" (Jn 8:58).

If no one else was aware of his divinity, demons were, and the evangelists recorded their testimony: "Have you come to destroy us? I know who you are, the Holy One of God" (Mk 1:24); "Whenever the unclean spirits saw him, they fell down before him and shouted, 'You are the Son of God'" (Mk 3:11);

"He shouted at the top of his voice, 'What have you to do with me, Jesus, Son of the Most High God?'" (Mk 5:7). If his own men were slow on the uptake, his enemies—the religious establishment and the Power of Darkness—read him loud and clear.

He frequently and unabashedly told people their sins were forgiven. He treated the Temple and the Sabbath as if he owned them. He respected the Law but never let it encroach on kindness. In the Sermon on the Mount, he kept drilling it like an evangelical preacher: "You have heard it said . . . but *I* tell you . . ." (MATTHEW 5) He said, right out: "Something greater than the Temple . . . greater than Solomon. . . . greater than Jonah is here" (MATTHEW 12).

Can we finally be rid of the mealy-mouthed, cowardly claim: "He was a beautiful moral teacher like Socrates, but . . ." The man claimed—and his disciples died rather than deny—that he was equal to the Creator. If he was not, he was either a lunatic or a liar. If he told the truth, we have no decent response other than bending the knee and declaring that Jesus Christ is Lord.

Thoughts to Ponder

Judas

Who could fathom his feelings? Paralyzing, immobilizing, overwhelming sadness. Let no one pass judgment who hasn't personally, seriously given thought to self-destruction quickly by suicide, endlessly by addiction. Cain felt it when he heard God call: "The voice of your brother's blood cries to me from the earth." Some Fathers of the Church implied that the brother of OT patriarch Joseph, Judah, sold him to the Ismaelites for thirty pieces of silver. Judas echoes the suicide of Ahitophel who betrayed the first David (2 SAM 17:23). Origen argued that his suicide was the act of a distraught soul seeking mercy the only way he knew how.

But it is easy to overlook the fact that Judas wasn't the only apostate and traitor among the first chosen. Both Peter and Judas are "foils" to the character of Jesus. Their cowardice and weakness sharpen our realization of Jesus' courage and steadfastness. One difference in their treacheries is that Judas's was premeditated. He had days to let decency simmer to the surface of whatever reasons he believed justified his act of betrayal. Peter's "motive"—as it was so often—was ill considered, emotional. Less a breach of faith than a failure of moral courage. Impossible that, in the lapses between his temptations, his subconscious didn't wrench his heart. But each twinge lifted him closer to the truth.

And the critical difference wasn't in their heads but in their guts. Peter "knew" he could be forgiven. Judas was certain he could never be. It is idiotic to force a limit on God's mercy.

[In that regard, Google "The Fullness of Time," by the Irish poet James Stephens.]

The Meaning of Power

That moment on the praetorium balcony juxtaposes three dramatically different embodiments of power: Pilate, Caiphas, and Jesus. Coercive, strictly secular power, equally coercive "spiritual" power, and the power in Jesus who wins—ultimately—by surrendering.

An impish thought: What might happen if all the needlepointers in the world fashioned samplers of the Beatitudes and we hung them on the inner side of stall doors in the rest rooms of all the congresses, parliaments, and politburos on Earth—in all the executive suits, all ad agencies' johns, even the bathrooms of the Roman Curia?

As I say, a mere impish whimsy.

Pope Francis exhorted us to "appreciate small things inside

larger horizons." The critical question is, "How large will I personally allow my horizons to expand?"

A second query: Must those three uses of power be, by their nature, mutually exclusive?

Honesty

Test this: The ultimate root of human morality is honesty, yielding to the truth, whatever the cost. No one will ever be genuinely unhappy who refuses ever to lie—to themselves.

12. The Place Called Skull

Yom Shishi (Friday)—About Noon

It was nearly midday when the charade of the king's triumphal enthronement began its royal procession from the Roman praetorium. They brought the prisoner up from the cellars with two other faceless villains and hauled them down from the balcony to the street leading to the northwest gate, shoving the onlookers against the walls of the stinking streets. Each prisoner had four handlers to prevent any malingering or temptations to bolt. Then came the centurion. Finally, the executioners, who had their equipment and knew their business.

The professionals had already hauled out the crosspieces. Planed logs a hand's length thick and a hand's length wide, like you'd bar a big door with, a foot longer than the average man's wingspan. Maybe a hundred pounds each. Uprights were already planted in Skull Hill.

In other countries, civilized places, the condemned were brought out naked the way the curs should be, if you're going to do the job right. It was supposed to be a warning, right? No other reason to drag it out. Or even do it. But these Jews thought skin was disgusting, not just whatever's inside. Like they were going for tea with the empress in the garden, la-di-da. The two bandits were looking fit for the fair, as they say, but the preacher was a bloody mess. He was substituting for some rebel named Barabbas. There was some kind of notice tacked to his beam, but no one could read what it said. And he'd been so messed up that, when they hiked the crosspiece onto his shoulder, it dropped him right to his knees. But he grunted himself to his feet, give him that. The blood patches on his tunic kept oozing larger.

As they pushed along the narrow alleyways, the veterans assigned to the boring duty jostled aside the shopkeepers shielding their stalls. Food, souvenirs, currency exchange. From over the Temple walls, you could already hear the screams of the thousands of animals lined up to get their throats cut for the pilgrims, who were bringing their life's savings from all over the world. And already the stink from burning guts. From up ahead at the gate you could hear the god-awful groaning from droves of more animals being herded into the city for sacrificial death. The walls and cobbles were crusted in slops and the crap from all the animals.

The problems would start when all the wogs got news of it. Didn't matter who the one going to dance the air was. Whoever. It was a spark of interest in their dead-end lives. Today, a bonus: Three at once. The preacher king and two thugs dumb enough to get caught slipping shanks into strangers in a riot. Whatever.

It was barely a half-mile to the gate and out to the old quarry. Hardly a fifteen-minute walk, but the prophet kept stumbling and falling, letting the crosspiece roll, dragging himself back up again. And his four handlers having to hoist the damn thing back up on his shoulder, all rusty and red with blood. It was going to take like forever. If that kept up, they'd all be dead before they got to the hill. So as they pulled up to the Damascus Gate, the centurion grabbed some big Jew out of the crowd of pilgrims and herdsmen and pickpockets.

"You, Big Jew!" the centurion said, clutching a fistful of the guy's tunic. "Whatcher name? You from around here?"

"Simon," the man said. "Africa. Not here."

"Good!" the centurion said. "Don't know who to complain to. Simon, ol' pal, you just won the lottery. You been picked from all these nice folks to serve the great Roman Empire. We got a package to deliver. Law says I can honor you by asking you to carry my load for a mile. Yes? Well, I'm telling you to heft this big log just a few hundred paces, maybe. Down into that quarry, see? Where that knob sticks up? Like a skull? With the poles sticking up out of its head? Big lug like you? A skip through the daisies!"

Big Simon looked helplessly around at the crowd of strangers. Not knowing what else to do, he squatted down and hoisted up one end of the big log. So the whole sad procession lurched into movement again, the prisoner on one end of the crosspiece, the big African Jew on the other.

A group of women edged along between the procession and the seething shopkeepers, weeping and beseeching their God. At least it sounded like prayers, and they shook their clasped hands at the sky. Always a few stray women. Mothers, sisters, live-ins, but some of these had odd accents, even if the soldiers couldn't understand most of their gibberish.

Jesus was saying, "Daughters, don't mourn for me. Weep for yourselves and for your children." He kept gouging for breath. "Mourn for what your leaders have done—as if it were your choice. If they light a fire so easily of green wood like me, how easily the fire will devour deadwood. But God won't reject you because those men have rejected me."

And on they trudged. All imprisoned in the only pace the battered guy could manage.

They turned from the northwest corner of the great city wall where the ground sloped down into an old quarry. At one side tombs had been hollowed from the rock faces, ringed by clumps of greenery that might once have been a garden. Many caves held the remains of men crucified on the knob humping up from the other end of the depression, knotted with scrub, men whose families—or confederates—could afford better than common graves in the Potter's Field down beyond the south wall. Usually, the remains stayed until nothing was left but bones, which could then be packed into a smaller stone ossuary, leaving the space open for further rental. These soldiers were nothing like the wogs standing around the hillock gaping. They wore scarlet skirts and light summer armor. Coarse, brutish, red hair, blackened teeth, sunburned faces yelling a tongue few understood, but the gogglers knew it was cursing. They dragged the crosspieces from the criminals' shoulders, then ripped off their clothes—except for the loincloths, to keep peace with the prissy Jews. Tougher on the preacher. His long splotched gown had already crusted itself into the ribbons of his skin. But he didn't yell. Just sort of cringed.

Their handlers shoved a sponge soaked in harsh poor-man's wine at each criminal's face. It was laced with some kind of drug, not from any womanish sentiment but, like everything else about this business, it was easier on the executioners. Prisoners could drink it if they wanted or be damned. The two rebels sucked it down eagerly. The preacher spat it out.

Then they stretched out all three rebels on the gravelly ground, which was also harder on the King of the Jews, what with his whole back and both legs raw meat in the dirt.

The whole process is easier to understand if you strip away any whim some artist might have and realize it was governed by the crude needs of the executioners. The purpose of the event wasn't necessarily sadistic, to prolong some kind of atonement for any crime. Instead, it was a salutary warning to any passerby tempted to some kind of antisocial behavior. Sometimes, the powers-that-be wanted hundreds crucified at once. Any professional carpenter would know it was a waste of time—not to mention impossible, knowing how the ignorant bosses wanted everything done yesterday—to hack and plane and sand a clean mortise slot for the crosspiece in the permanent upright.

So the rough-cut beam was simply set on top of the upright in a T and nailed temporarily in place. Ropes were too time-consuming. Nails were more efficient, besides saving a day of endless, useless dying if they used ropes. The upright poles were low, maybe eight or nine feet depending on the local wood supply. That way, those crucified for the beasts in an arena were accessible when the animals were let loose to savage them. When victims were exposed by the roadside, wolves tended to the remains. Even more important than disposal of the corpse, a short pole meant the four handlers were enough to lift the crosspiece and the criminal to the top. Who would lug some kind of ladder out every time some scum got stuck up there?

A little shelf to hold up the buttocks and a wedge for the feet depended on your carpenter. Or the number of crosses when the area was first set up. The ledges kept the nails from splitting through the wrists from the prisoner's full weight, especially if the victim was some kind of fat hog, but it gave the condemned a chance to lift himself up and get a breath. Which only dragged the whole business out unnecessarily.

Once the three rebels were stretched out, it took the executioners a bit of time, measuring first where to open a starting hole with an augur at the length of each prisoner's wrists. The nails were as long as a woman's hand, but the executioner, whose trade this was, could usually make it bite all the way into the wood with one good blow of his mallet. Each was driven in where the wrist joined the heel of the rictused hand, then the feet, nailed flat to the upright when there was no small shelf. The two others shrieked like butchered bulls. The preacher bit his cheeks.

The big handlers lifted each crosspiece with its attached victim, maybe 250 pounds for four soldiers—but awkward. They carried it to the upright shaft, lifted it to their arms' length, and dropped it heavily on top, one of the army carpenters angling a long nail in from the back to keep it from slipping. The moment they let go, the preacher's body dropped a foot, hanging the entire weight of his body on his wrists, exposing the title crudely written just above and behind his thorny head: *Jesus Nazarenus, Rex Judaeorum.*

That little frill caused an unholy stink from the priggish priests.

Which was precisely why Pilate had ordered it, wrenching away their hour of triumph. It was as much an insult to priests and people as to the one they'd condemned. It said, "This is the king the Jews deserve!" Caiphas and the others sent word to the governor demanding it be taken off. "Instead, write, 'He *claimed* to be King of the Jews.'" Pilate sent the reply: "What I've written, I've written."

Jesus sagged, reaching deep into his guts to get breath into his cramped lungs. It seemed he needed to say something. Flies busily drank the blood from his wounds and the tears from the corners of his eyes, swollen and purpled. His nose was broken. His thumbs and fingers jerked involuntarily toward his palms. There was no space for any more pain.

Jesus raised his head against the ache in his neck, driving the thorns further into his scalp. He rasped out: "Father, forgive them. They don't know what they're doing."

Not many heard him, and of those who did, few felt much need of what he offered.

Beyond the agonies in every part of himself, there was no lack of reminders of his failure. Hearing who it was, passersby on the northern road to the gate snorted, "He's the one gonna tumble the Temple down the cliff, right?" Another said, "I heard he thinks he's the Son of God." Yet another snickered, "Your Son of God seems to be havin' some trouble tumblin' his ass off that cross!" The eldest clerical dignitaries and a few priests not assigned to the wholesale animal slaughter in the Temple up on the mountain sniggered, "He saved so many! Doesn't seem too clever at saving himself, does he? . . . Oh, Messiah! . . . Oh, Son of David! . . . King of Israel! Show us your power! . . . Descend from your throne! Give us proof! So we can *believe!*"

The Roman soldiers joined in, halfheartedly. Earlier, in the courtyard, they'd had the spirit for it. Now it was just stinking work.

One of the rebels crucified next to Jesus lifted his head, a string of slobber hanging from the corner of his mouth. "Hey," he snarled. "Hey, *Messiah*! Hey, you dumb jackass!"

The detail of soldiers squatted down and began to toss dice for the clothes, sharing their crude skin canteens, loosening their fittings. All over but the god-awful tedious wait.

"Hey, you!" the angry rebel hollered again. "Look over here, you phoney!"

Jesus seemed to be trying to turn his head.

"Ho, boy!" the man hooted. "I waited for *you* from when I was a kid, Holy Messiah! Now, how 'bout you pull off a . . ." He heaved for another breath. "Pull off a messiah miracle for . . . us. *Huh?*" The breath rasped from his tortured lungs. The rant seemed worth the pain. "Get us all . . . down from here, you dumb . . . *Sowson!*"

The other rebel turned and rasped across Jesus. "Shut your damn mouth, you halfwit!"

"*Make* me!" the other hollered.

"Don't you even fear God?" the second one growled. He waited for breath. "Leave him alone, for . . . luvva God! He didn't do . . . nothin'. He don't . . . belong here . . . like us."

"Let luvva God . . . get him down . . . then! *And* me, while . . . at it! Son of a cross-eyed sow!"

The second one called out. "Hey, Jesus!"

Jesus tried to twist his head to that side. He blinked to the second rebel. "Jesus," the second man coughed. "Don't mind him, huh? . . . When you get to . . . to this fancy kingdom o' yours, say . . . say hello for me, wouldja? To any my pals . . . the one or two that crapped . . . all over the odds . . . and got there?"

Jesus sucked up breath. "Today," he gasped. "Today. You'll . . . " He coughed. "You'll be there . . . too . . . with me. My word . . . on it."

It happened so gradually few had been aware of it. The sky had gone dark. Almost like an eclipse. But that was impossible at full moon. Or like a sudden sandstorm from the south. But there was no real wind. As if the world had stopped breathing. Something else then. Whatever. It was unnerving. The crowd was beginning to thin out, not just because of the baleful sky. They had to get ready for the Sabbath. And the feast. Besides, it was all over now but the waiting. For the three to let go. No diversion left.

Huddled below the central cross were a man and three women named Mary. One was the wife of Cleophas, a man some said was Jesus' paternal uncle. One was Magdalene, out of whom Jesus had cast seven devils. One was his mother. The man was John, the idealist, the dreamer.

Jesus hacked and gargled, "Mother." She wrenched her face up to him. "John . . . will be . . . your son." She nodded. "Son!" The young man's eyes reached upward. "Son," Jesus went on, nodding toward his mother. "She's . . . your mother now."

It was three hours into the whole sorry business, heat lightning began to gash the unnatural midnight sky. Jesus strained against the nails, like a chained beast. He threw back his head and sent a desperate scream up into the darkness. "*Eli! Eli! Eli!*" he cried.

That unexpected shout from a corpse jerked all the soldiers' heads up to the central cross. One of them grabbed a Jewish carpenter's arm. "Wha'd he say?"

"The prophet Elijah. He's calling for him."

Jesus' mouth gaped wider and he shrieked the rest: "My God! My God! *God! Why?* Why have you *deserted* me?"

A young soldier picked up his skin canteen and said, "Eli's their word for God. He's calling God." He looked around for a rag and a stick or something to slake the man's thirst. So they could understand.

The first man batted him back. "Leave him be. Maybe his god'll show *up*! Wouldn't that be a pisser? Or maybe this *real* prophet, Eli. Give 'em a chance!"

But Jesus croaked again, "*Ana sameh!*"

The young soldier biffed the carpenter's shoulder. "What?"

The Jew grunted, "He's thirsty."

The boy grabbed a rag from the small pile he'd won dicing. He soaked it with sour wine from his canteen, put it onto the point of his spear, and poked it up into Jesus' mouth. Jesus closed his lips on it and finally swallowed.

"Father, into your hands I offer my soul." Then, softer than a sigh, Jesus said: "*Done!*"

His head dropped, and the Son of God gave up the ghost and died.

The sacrificial cup he had pleaded to evade was drunk dry.

The surly centurion grabbed the wineskin and slobbered down a mouthful, raking his hairy forearm over his lips. He looked up at the corpse. "That bastard was a son of God," he growled.

A story got round that, at that very minute, there was a kind of earthquake, but nobody else found that worth writing down. And they said the great sixty-foot tapestry at the door of the inmost Temple, which separated the vile world from the place where the coruscating presence of God hovered, was ripped right down the middle, no tougher than a spider web. They said, too, that graves in the vast necropolis south of the Mount of Olives cracked open, and the greatest souls in Hebrew history broke out from living death in Sheol, freed by the death of God.

But what fool could swallow that?

Orders from the top. The pushy priests had given Pilate no peace. So to get the vultures out of his head, he changed the usual procedure of letting Fate snip off the lives of the condemned. A strong man would last two, three days. Ordinarily, they left the bodies for crows, flies, and any dogs that could jump high enough. But he ordered all three should be strangled or have their legs broken or anyway disposed of so they wouldn't be a blot on the damn Passover.

So the soldiers got the executioners to batter the rebels' legs, shock the life out of them. But when they came to the middle cross, the prophet was already dead. So, with oxen obedience, one of them grabbed a spear and stabbed him in the heart. There was almost no blood left.

But at last the whole travesty was over.

The quarry was now deserted. A pious wealthy Jew named Joseph, a member of the high council, one of the few who hadn't approved the action against Jesus, had already gone to Pilate and formally requested permission to remove the corpse as soon as possible. It would lessen tensions, he said, if the teacher were entombed privately rather than dumped with the two others in a common ditch. He offered his own tomb, hewn from the nearby rock face, at least temporarily. Pilate, as dubious of an afterlife as any Sadducee, was only too willing to approve.

Meanwhile, before the shops were shuttered, another councilor named Nicodemus, who had visited Jesus secretly, bought the needed spices and the burial cloth. Because the Sabbath and feast were almost upon them, the anointing would have to wait a full day. But it was unfitting that such a person as Jesus be merely left naked in a cave.

Two of Joseph's men looped the burial sheet under the arms, and one of the men anchored the knees below. Then began the whole wretched task of drawing out the nails and lowering the corpse into the hands of two others, who draped it onto the shroud stretched across the knees of his mother. The other women tucked a kerchief across the face, then carefully folded the other half of the long cloth over the head, down the battered length of the body, and tied it around his ankles.

His mother reluctantly yielded her burden. The women followed the bearers so they might come back again after the Sabbath to bathe away the blood and anoint the body.

At the tomb, the men laid the corpse on a rock shelf and eased back out into the somber twilight. With some effort, they rolled the rounded stone along its narrow track and covered the opening. Silently, in twos and threes, they drifted back toward the northwest gate.

Lamps were lit in the Temple. The trumpeter declared the feast had begun.

And so, at least for the moment, it was finished.

Puzzling Moments

Crucifixion

After the Spartacus Revolt in 71 BCE, six thousand crosses lined the road from Capua to Rome. Cicero called it *crudelissimum et teterrimum supplicium*, "very cruelest and utterly terrifying punishment." It was so barbarous that anyone who had witnessed it ordinarily refused to discuss it, like veterans from modern wars. Yet *all four* evangelists describe it in absolutely undramatic terms, simply, "They crucified him." No ringing of mallets, no spurts of blood as in modern films. One reason for their restraint could have been that this manner of death was so utterly degrading, it gave one more reason to despise a new cult that worshiped a crucified felon.

On the other hand, it might have been that the Gospel writers were convinced that, at this point, the story was not yet over.

Many Marys

Possibly because the sister of Moses was Miriam, there are too many Marys in the final scenes of the Gospel for even the experts to differentiate them. Thus I bow before an impregnable knot. However, the four inspired authors found no justification in merely inventing names, which argues for the likelihood they bowed to consistent eyewitness reports.

Moreover, it seems to underline unequivocally that males were embarrassingly absent and that females were the most fearless and stalwart original disciples. Magdalene is reported by all four, and she is the first person to preach *the* good news of the resurrection.

His Mother

Mary the mother of Jesus appears at the cross only in John, likely for more theological than reportorial reasons. There is no mention of the men laying Jesus' body on her knees, but *The Pieta* is "evidence" enough for me. The last mention of her in the Synoptics was when she and his "family" came seeking him and were left outside (MARK 3; MATTHEW 12; LUKE 8).

The theological symbolisms of her presence begin with the earliest church fathers and run freely still. She is the New Eve at the death/birth of the new age, she is the Mother of the Church (symbolized by John). Whether that was the intention of the author(s) of the Fourth Gospel or not, the symbolism is still "fitting." Like the godparents at a baptism, Mary and John are the guides of the new community. (A snarky insight: Neither was a trained thinker.)

"The Beloved Disciple"

Nowhere in the Gospels is this vague personage identified. He could be the Apostle John, who seemed to have an affectionate relationship with Jesus at the Last Supper (reduced to the absurd by *The Da Vinci Code*). This evasive figure occurs a half-dozen times in John: sitting next to Jesus at the supper; "known to the high priest [Annas]," thus securing Peter's entrance to the courtyard; here at the cross; along with Peter the one to whom the risen Jesus sends Magdalene; one of the seven when the risen Jesus causes the miraculous draft of fish ("It's the Lord!"); and finally, at the very end, Jesus says he intends this "disciple" to "remain until I come."

Eusebius (260–340) records a claim by Polycrates one hundred years earlier that John the Apostle was both "the beloved disciple" and the author of the Fourth Gospel. Few moderns agree.

Since (as far as we know) Jesus hasn't made his final appearance on Earth, and we assume the Apostle John has died, "the beloved disciple" might not be the Apostle John.

He was likely not John the Evangelist either, despite the note in the very last verses (Jn 21:24): "This is the disciple who is testifying to these things and has written them, and we know that his testimony is true." From those words alone, we know that the whole Gospel we have in our hands at the moment was passed on by that "we," yet in some way their testimony is validated by an eyewitness. Who? Depends on your scholar. Some fasten on the hope that this "disciple" could be any individual where the Gospels put the words "Jesus" and "loved" together.

Some have proposed Lazarus of Bethany, even Magdalene. In *The Passover Plot*, Hugh J. Schonfield imagines this "disciple" to be a highly placed Temple priest unable to follow Jesus openly, like Joseph of Arimathea or Nicodemus. Another candidate is "James," mentioned more than once as a "brother" of Jesus— which, of course, would explain a literal (if unnecessary) reason for "behold your mother." Catholics then had to find another tangent, by suspecting the word meant "cousin" or that Joseph had been widowed with other children or that Mary was a virgin only until after her *"first* born." Which seems to require too much clever dancing.

Colm Toibin, in his ugly novel/play *The Testament of Mary,* even pictures the source of this Gospel as Jesus' mother, and a bitter old Irish woman at that. One could as easily offer as this "disciple" the rich young man invited but unable to become an apostle (Mk 10:17-21), since the text says Jesus "loved him" simply for living a godly life. How important is it?

A reason for the lack of specification of this "beloved disciple" could well be security. If the author were personally identified, he (or she) could have been instantly arrested. Literarily, at each appearance this "disciple" acts as a "foil" for Simon Peter. Another real possibility is that the author(s) wanted any reader to identify with this follower. To "remain until I come."

In any case, the fog surrounding this one figure hardly justifies distrust of the Gospels.

God Near Despair

Here, Jesus doesn't say, "Father," his usual expression for his relationship with the Divinity, but "My *God!*" The contrast is meaningful. What Jesus is enduring at the moment simply defies the magnanimous character embodied in the father of the prodigal son or the shepherd who leaves the ninety-nine. Not to mention the compassionate Jesus of a few hours before: "They don't know what they're doing." This is *God.* The one whom the observer (at least at this juncture) views as on the one hand the impassive, distant *Ipsum Esse Subsistens* and the serenely indifferent Ultimate of Eastern religions, but at the same time the chthonic, bloodlusting Moloch who demands torment in atonement.

If there is any element in my own faith that catalyzes me as Christian rather than any other kind of theist, it is this moment. The *scandal* of the cross. This is not the stoic Socrates blithely reaching for the hemlock. This is "Do not go gentle into that good night. Rage, rage against the dying of the light." This is Job, bellowing chapter after chapter at the cosmic unfairness. Virgil's *lachrymae rerum*. Mistah Kurtz gargling: "The horror! The horror!" Beckett's Vladimir hearing the little boy assuring him, "Mr. Godot told me to tell you he won't come this evening but surely tomorrow." Peggy Lee's "Is that all there is?" Abandonment.

Like us—like me—this battered God felt hurt by loneliness, slander, misunderstanding, failure, treachery. "He descended into hell." Not literally, of course. But he scoured the utter bottom of the humans-only abyss. He shuddered at the silence of the One he still clung to.

Hebrews (5:8) says, "He learned obedience by *yielding* to suffering." The answer to the conundrum of Calvary isn't atonement to an implacable Enemy. It's a lesson in loving surrender —which are often coterminous—God showing us "how it's done."

It is worth belaboring again: Ancient Job could have looked up at the Whirlwind God and justly asked, "Do you have any idea how this *feels*? Or do you know it only as an idea, as a male pretends to understand the agony and love in childbirth?" Here at the foot of the cross, Job can offer the same querulous complaint, and God can look back down and say, "Yes, Job. Now I do know how it *feels*."

I can rejoice in a God who felt *godforsaken*.

If you can't deal with paradox, you landed in the wrong universe.

Special Effects

Especially Matthew delights in underlining the message by animating the scene with flashes and explosions. (A modern concert goes even further. The Narnia and Lord of the Rings films dramatize the underlying battle between Good and Evil in much the same way, because in a world like ours Evil is so glamorized few see the poison beneath the seductive surfaces.)

As with the rollicking angelic chorus at the nativity, nature shows empathy at the death of God in this episode—darkness at noon and an earthquake and the sundering of the tough fabric masking the old Holy of Holies and the undead roaming the Jerusalem streets—none of which anyone else recorded. It captures again the conflict between "accurate" and meaningful." The believer whose faith rests in connection to a Person rather than on-site cameras or the assertions of a catechism says, "If it didn't 'really' happen, it *should* have." Nature *should* have been revolted. So should I be. And grateful.

The Centurion

Till now, the only vocal testimony to the divinity of Jesus no matter what that objectively entails came from *demons*. The very first human being to testify to it—again, no matter what the character meant or even if he actually said those words—was a tough, battle-scarred pagan.

This victim had been betrayed by Judas, abandoned by all of his friends, denied by Peter, condemned for blasphemy by the priests, rejected by the mob, mocked by a king, the priests, soldiers who had no idea or care of who he was, passersby, a fellow convict. But "something" led Mark to place this incredible, highly theological claim in the mouth of a Roman centurion.

Jesus' divine sonship has been the whole developmental theme of Mark's Gospel. The gradual revelation of that unique relationship is called "The Messianic Secret," ever so gradually revealed. "Who are you?" Mark has Peter ease back the covering: "You are the Messiah" (Mk 8:29), but Jesus bade them not to tell anyone. "To you has been given the secret of the kingdom of God, but for those outside, everything comes in parables" (Mk 4:11). After the transfiguration, "he ordered them to tell no one about what they had seen, until after the Son of Man had risen from the dead" (Mk 9:9). The crescendo began edging toward a climax when Caiphas, the high priest, bound Jesus under solemn oath: "Are you the Messiah, the Son of the Blessed One?" and Jesus finally replied, unhesitatingly, "I *am!*" (Mk 14:61-62). Finally, here: "Truly this man was God's Son!" (Mk 15:39), from the pagan who oversaw his execution.

Even after the staggering experiences of Jesus risen, the disciples took a long time even to accept some completely undefined concept of who Jesus really was. In fact, it took the best minds in Christendom centuries to come to still-inadequate "explanation." Today, after *twenty* centuries, few firmly convinced Christians would face a firing squad for "consubstantial."

Burial

Deuteronomy demands: "When someone is convicted of a crime punishable by death and is executed, and you hang him on a tree, his corpse must not remain all night upon the tree; you shall bury him that same day, for anyone hung on a tree is under God's curse"

(21:22-23). The usual Roman practice was to leave the victims to nature, time, the elements, but this was the eve of the great feast, the religious officials wanted to get the disgusting reminder out of sight, and Joseph of Arimathea had enough clout to petition the governor and relieve him of an odious task. What's more, everything concerning death was *tref,* unclean, to be handled as expeditiously as possible, especially with the Sabbath and the feast fast approaching.

Joseph and Nicodemus were courageous men, daring the contempt of fellow Sanhedrists. They are examples of once-hesitant believers, and their names were probably remembered because they were converted. The spices—myrrh, balsam, aloes—were intended to offset the inevitable smell of decay. But the best they could offer in the rush before the Sabbath was a quick covering with the shroud. There was no water to wash the body or time to anoint it. All would have to wait a day. In almost all English versions, John says Nicodemus brought "a hundred pounds" of spices (JN 19:39), which beggars imagination. A. J. Jannaris proposes reading *hekaston* (a pound) rather than *hekaton* (a hundred). Another occasion where a single Greek letter makes a difference, however small.

Elements to Ponder

"Father, Forgive"

Even if someone could prove Luke or some later copyist dared insert it, this one stunning sentence probably sums up Christian behavior as well as any single sentence could. It was an inescapable theme—forgiveness and a new life: adulterous woman, wayward son, lost sheep, people whose more evident problems were paralysis and skin-rot, "as we forgive those who trespass against us," "seventy times seven times," "pray for those who persecute you." Not to mention the first pope and bishops who apostatized, denied Christ within hours of their first Mass.

One amazing parish has—right on the front page of their bulletin: "Welcome! Even if you're unbaptized, divorced, gay, confused, sinful, lost. So are we. You're welcome here." I have a hunch that, if one of the easily befuddled first disciples were to be transported to today, he'd nod, and maybe sigh, and say, "Yep. That's what *he* did, too. Like this whore one time. Right in the middle of dinner, in this really classy home, she comes in and sobs on his feet and wipes them with her hair. It was *so* embarrassing! And he *kept* doin' that!"

It's not the music, or the rubrics, or the orthodoxy. It's the welcome. The heart.

The Kind Rebel

There is nothing in the Scripture I can discover that justifies calling this man "repentant." To do so undercuts the whole point, purposely ignored by neopuritans. This criminal did not "*gain* heaven" (which is Pelagianism) by a single word of self-reproach, no more than did the "woman known as a sinner" or the adulterous woman. Even the prodigal was embraced and kissed *before* he apologized. There isn't even any indication this man believed in this "kingdom" any more than the priests did. The evidence equally supports the view that he merely took pity on this poor deluded fool—who seemed so innocent and feckless.

He was welcomed simply because he was *kind*.

This, too, melds seamlessly into the general picture of the God embodied in Jesus. He insisted that the *only* question at the Final Judgment had *nothing* to do with sin (MATTHEW 25). The sole question will be: "Did you even notice me in the sufferers? How did you treat me then?"

The Temple Curtain

Like Gabriel's wingspan, the magi, the celestial nativity choir, walking on water, and the climactic earthquake, lack of outside evidence for the rending of the enormous Temple curtain should bother only those who still cling to Santa Claus or to the belief that all human turmoil—and death itself—can be laid at the feet of two inept nudists who were suckered by a talking snake. (Somehow serpents have lost that talent over the years.)

The torn curtain threw *open* the Most Holy Place on Earth, into which only an ordained priest could legitimately enter—and only once a year and by luck of a lottery. When Jesus gasps, "Done!" he means not just the *kairos*—the most critical moment since the creation—and the cup he had been so fearful of consuming were finished forever. Gone, now, also is the exclusivity of Judaism. Luther wrote, "Christ is the end of the Law. What it requires, Christ has performed."

"I Thirst"

It was a savage thirst from blood loss, with agonizing cramps in his limbs, his chest distended. All the symptoms of asphyxia: reddened face, body covered with sweat. The only other time in the Gospels Jesus ever asked for anything was a drink from the Samaritan woman at the well. He now finds himself in exactly the same torment as the rich man who pleaded with Abraham to send the leper to dip his finger in water and touch his tongue (LUKE 16).

"My mouth is dried up like a potsherd, and my tongue sticks to my jaws" (Ps 22:15).

To have even the slightest notion what this scene portrays try to remember that this is *God* talking. This is an incarnational thirst.

> Who, though he was in the form of God,
> did not regard equality with God
> as something to be exploited,
> but emptied himself,
> taking the form of a slave, being born in human likeness.
> And being found in human form,
> he humbled himself

and became obedient to the point of death—
even death on a cross. (Phil 2:6-10)

Immediately after his consecration of the cup at the Last Supper, Jesus said, "Truly, I say to you, I shall not drink again of the fruit of the vine until that day when I drink it new in the kingdom of God" (Mk 14:25).

This is that moment.

Yielding

Moderns seem convinced that "happiness" means having no significant problems and being "upbeat." The ancients were less shallow. For the Greeks happiness was not "feeling good" but "being good": *eudaimonia*, "having a good soul." In that understanding, Hitler capering at the Tomb of Napoleon over the humiliation of France wasn't happy, just feeling perky for the moment. In contrast, men and women striding to his gas chambers in Poland with their souls clasped firmly in their own two hands had found genuine happiness, success, fulfillment. The core of this moment is: "You can savage my body, but you can never usurp my soul."

Just so, imitation of Christ is "the way, the truth, and the life."

I lay down my life in order to take it up again.

No one takes it from me, but I lay it down of my own accord.

I have power to lay it down, and I have power to take it up again.

I have received this command from my Father. (Jn 10:17-20).

This is a way of looking at life never taught before: Victory through surrender.

13. The Longest Day

Shabbat (Saturday)

It was the worst Sabbath of their lives.

None of them dared leave the upstairs room. Who knew what more revenge the priests wanted? And it was the Sabbath. So they were forbidden to walk even as far as the Lazarus house in Bethany. The Temple would mean at the very least a flogging. Or prison. Or worse.

Some stretched out on the divans and pretended to sleep. Some squatted, each resolutely alone, along the walls. Simon hunkered under the stripped table, his prayer shawl draped over his head and his face. When someone tried to break the sullen silence: "Shouldn't we . . . ," he was rasped to silence. If someone began to pace, someone else just snapped, "*Stop* it!"

Even John, who'd been there, refused to talk about it after he'd said, "It's all over."

And it all was. Over.

Today was also Passover. The day of liberation. If belief in anything was still possible.

> He struck Egypt through their firstborn,
>   for his steadfast love endures forever;
> and brought Israel out from among them,
>   for his steadfast love endures forever;
> with a strong hand and an outstretched arm,

for his steadfast love endures forever;
who divided the Red Sea in two,
   for his steadfast love endures forever;
and made Israel pass through the midst of it,
   for his steadfast love endures forever.
(Ps 136:10-14)

But not us. We're no better than the priests. We fled the one we so firmly believed was the One Who Is to Come, the Holy One of God, *Mashiach*.

And so you have rejected us and abased us,
   and have not gone out with our armies.
You made us run away in shame from the foe,
   and our enemies have taken spoil for themselves.
You have made us like sheep for slaughter,
   and have scattered us among the nations. (Ps 44:9-11)

Each was imprisoned in his own skin, but the marauding thoughts were the same in each one's mind, swooping and twisting round and round. "Didn't he *tell* the guards to let us go? He *meant* us to go . . . I just didn't *think*! I just got caught up in the stampede . . . I hardly slept last night. This might have been a nightmare . . . It's just possible I wasn't even *there*."

And so it went. Hour after hour.

The women had laid out food last night before dark. No one wanted any.

The very worst part was not being able to escape one another. Or their own selves.

Maybe it was better to go out and be arrested. Maybe the only way away from the midnight hags in their heads was to die, too.

Maybe when it got dark they could sleep. Most likely not.

14. Openings

Yom Rishon (Very Early Sunday Morning)

Mary Magdalene scurried along the street at the earliest hint of dawn. She had made certain she could distinguish a white from a black thread, that the Sabbath and feast were clearly over and the work week had begun again. On one hip she carried a jug of water with a clean towel looped through the handle, on the other a flask with the funeral spices ready mixed. Only the most dedicated shopkeepers were already setting up their stalls along the street. The sun wasn't yet high enough to warm away the night chill.

She came up to the Damascus Gate and saw the Roman guards at their posts, yawning and scratching. The final night watch went from three to six. They made no move to stop her. The orders had been to stop "any *men*." And their relief was already overdue. When you've got a job, why go looking for work?

But the sight of them made her stop in her tracks.

Fool, she thought to herself. The stone. That evening it had taken three men.

She almost went back for help, but little chance any of the men could be lured out where anyone at all might recognize them. No one could tell one woman from another unless she were a hag or a whore.

I can sit, she thought. And wait. And pray. And he won't be alone.

She passed through the gate. The guards were too sleep-needful to be rude. She picked her way down the long slope into the overgrown area where the tombs stood, and she pushed her way through the brush to the path in front of the rich man's grotto.

Suddenly, she was again struck still, staring. Openmouthed. The flask slipped from her grip, and the crockery jug shattered on the rocks.

The round stone lay flat on the ground, cracked in two. The tomb gaped open.

Oh, no! Someone's taken him.

She turned on her heel, rucked up her skirts and began to run back up the slope to the gate. The guards stopped their fiddling and gaped, ready to jump whatever drunk fool from the graveyard was after her, but no one came. As she ran along the cobbles, merchants stopped their fussing, too, and wondered what could have gotten into this madwoman. Women don't run.

Mary burst through the street door of the hiding place, up the stairs, and hammered on the barred door of the room where the men were hiding. Young John opened it only a few inches, one eye peering out.

"Are they after you?" he choked.

"No, you fool. Get Simon! They've taken him away. Out of the tomb!" And she turned down the stairs again. She waited at the bottom for what seemed forever while John roused Simon Peter, who had said not a word to anyone since it happened.

"Come!" Mary shouted. "We have to find where they put him!"

The three ran along the street like fugitives. As they hurtled through the gates, the squad of guards still waiting their relief sprang up and hollered, "Halt! *Stop!*"

The three disciples stopped, poised to run again. "They've robbed the grave!" John shouted, and the three started away. Two guards set off in their wake. "Come back here!"

The woman and two men found the path through the brush and stood in front of the gaping hole. The two soldiers caught up with them, all five breathless. Uncertain what to do. What might be lurking inside a grave.

"By the gods," said one guard. "No way! I swear, no one came out of here last night!"

The older one pushed forward. "There was that god-awful storm. Great thunderclaps. They might have slipped by, no? And the noise? That young one was crapping his pants. Lightning couldn't have done that to that stone. Could it?"

John picked up his courage, bent down, and peered into the darkness. In the shadows, he saw the winding sheet in a heap. The cave empty. He backed out and gestured Peter in.

Peter stooped and pushed into the shallow cave. He saw the bloodstained shroud on the floor beneath the ledge. Oddly, the kerchief from the corpse's face was on the ledge, but folded carefully by itself, neatly. Who would steal a body and leave the grave cloths? What Jew would dare *tref*, touching a body so long dead?

The two backed into the gathering light. "Lightning didn't take his body," Simon said.

The older guard looked in and backed out, sputtering. "I'll cover the gate," he said to the other. "Go tell them back at the praetorium." And both ran up the incline to the gate.

John brushed past the astonished Peter, and put his head into the opening again, looking around in the dim emptiness. He smiled and spoke so softly the others failed to hear him. "He did it." Then he shook his head. Wishful thinking. The body was simply gone. But how? Why?

The two men moved disconsolately out of the gloom. Mary stood with tears brimming in her eyes and dribbling down her cheeks. She looked with brief hope at the others. Her fist went to her mouth as she realized the men were as baffled as she was.

Peter and John trudged up the long slope to the gate, leaving

Mary standing outside the tomb, like Lot's wife. Her mind was utterly blank. There had to be an answer.

She stooped and for the first time actually looked into the empty cavern herself.

But it wasn't empty. Or her brain was fevered.

There were two *presences*. Radiances. Hovering over the ledge, one at the head, the other at the foot. One spoke. "Woman," it said, in a voice like music. "Why are you crying?"

"Our teacher," she faltered. "They've taken him away. I don't know where to find him."

Bewildered, she turned to leave. But a man stood in her way. "Woman," he said, exactly like the angel, "Why are you crying?"

She twitched in surprise. The caretaker. "Oh, *sir*!" she said. "If you took him . . . please! Tell me where. So I can bring him back. I *have* to bring him back!"

The man said, very softly, "Mary."

Magdalene's fist struck her heart. And she knew. "Teacher," she breathed and fell to her knees, grasping his legs.

He caught her elbows, lifting her to her feet again. "Don't cling. I'm here. I'm here for a time. At least like this. So. Go to my brothers, yes? And Peter. Tell them."

And, suddenly, the solidity of him was simply no longer there.

Once again, in a delirium of doubt and disbelief and utter certainty, she ran up the hill, past the astonished guards, through the gate and onto the long cobbled street to the house where the apostles were hiding. She slammed through the door, grabbed her skirts to run up the stairs. She hammered on the door. And hammered.

"I've seen him!" she cried. "I've seen him! He's *alive* again!"

Again, John opened the door carefully, his face agape. They were all sitting around the upper room, dumbfounded as she rattled on wildly about the shining presences, the voice, the caretaker, the feel of his legs.

And of course they didn't believe a word of it. Hysterical woman.

In the late afternoon, the people from downstairs had left them wine and food, and the men had barred the door behind them. The Magdalene, sputtering and hammering at their chests and shoulders because they refused to believe her nonsense, went down with them. . . .

When she had first come back, she had stirred a tornado of responses, cynical, scowling, half-hopeful, ultimately derisive. She'd been possessed once, hadn't she? Seven devils? Unstable. Yes, he *had* spoken of it. Rising again. But later. Much, much later. Centuries.

And half the rabbis said even that was a delusion. Yes, they'd believed it themselves. Awhile. Simply because they'd so desperately wanted to believe it. To believe that life could be larger than the day-after-day frustrations and resentments and predictable defeats. Like this.

They'd left home for him. Risked everything that meant anything. Even their faith.

Then again. What if—what if impossibly—it were true? They'd run. They'd left him alone. With the venomous priests and the brutal police. How could they dare face him if this was true?

But if he had *really* been who they'd begun to believe he was, he *could* have saved himself. Surely. He'd done it before. At the very beginning, when the Nazareth men were ready to hurl him off the cliff. He just walked right through them. Like Moses through the Red Sea. And last winter, on Solomon's porch, when the locals had picked up rocks to stone him because they thought he was making himself into God. And they tried to arrest him? He just walked away like a priest from beggars.

He could have done it in the garden. When they ran. But he'd *told* them to. Practically.

Now some madmen had taken his corpse. What possible brain-sick reason? The last thing the priests would have tolerated. Not the Romans. Some perverted sect? Had Jesus infuriated anyone else? Too many to choose from.

And round and round and forward and backwards and up and down until they'd exhausted all arguments, all tolerance, all hope for meaning. One another. Finally, they all eased back into the dark torpor they'd sulked in for days.

Later, not one of them—not a single one—could find words for what happened next.

From out of nowhere, there he *was.*

But radiant. Hard to look straight at. His gown woven of light.

There was no way to test it. Or need to. He was as real as you know bread and wine are real, without need to taste or touch them.

He said, very quietly, "Peace." He held out his wrists. They saw the holes, healed. He parted the gown at the neck and showed them the scar over his heart. They could hardly breathe.

"Now," he said. "The mission is yours. As the Father sent me to you, I send you. My Spirit is now breathed into you. Take it out to the whole world. Forgive those who regret and repent. Those who refuse you, refuse love."

Then he went to Peter, crouching disconsolately by the wall, terrified, simply unable to look up. Jesus reached down, took his elbows as he had Magdalene, and raised him up. He looked into Peter's frightened, tear-filled eyes. Then he wrapped his arms around him. Tight.

And then he was gone. Just not there anymore. And yet . . .

That same evening, a couple of hours before dark, Cleophas, Jesus' uncle, and his wife, Mary, who'd been at the cross, were making their way unhappily toward Emmaus, a town seven miles north-west of the city at the end of Ayalon Valley. Two hours' walk. An overnight stopover on their long journey back to Galilee. Get a leg of the journey out of the way. More importantly, get away from the cauldron of Jerusalem and its destruction of their profoundest hopes. The open road was more dangerous after dark, but it was a place to breathe and to unburden themselves of the shattered illusions they dared not broach in the city, even in whispers.

Arguing, as spouses sometimes do. Mary was cautiously exuberant, hoping the news was true—and more important, rerooting their hopes. The tomb was definitely empty. Even stubborn Simon admitted that. And, say what you want about the Magdala woman, she was there when they killed him. Mary had been there herself. And Magdalene had also *seen* him. Well, then? "And don't give me that 'she's only a woman!' She was there before any man!"

Cleophas was sourly convinced it was all over. So they had almost tired of snapping at one another, rehashing "And what will we do now?"

Suddenly, she put her hand on her husband's arm to silence him. "Someone's back there," she whispered. They stopped, and Cleophas moved in front of his wife and lifted his stout staff at an angle in front of them, ready.

The stranger was a big man, and the couple tensed. But he was alone. The sky was darkening. The village inn was only a bit up the road. But neither of them could outrun him.

The man raised his hand. "Hello!" he hollered. "I'm alone. Don't be afraid. I mean you no harm. May I join you?"

He approached slowly, hands empty in the air. The couple was stiffly wary, angling their eyes around him in case there were others.

"My name is Cleophas," the man volunteered, cautiously. "This is my wife, Mary."

"Are you on your way north?"

"Eventually."

"Thank you for letting me walk with you," the stranger said. "It gets lonely."

"Yes," the woman murmured, still watchful, uncomfortable.

"Forgive me. In the silence I couldn't help hearing. You seemed to be mourning. I hope I'm not interfering."

Cleophas replied, "This weekend. The teacher. We had such hopes." He fought the tears.

"Teacher?" the stranger echoed.

"Jesus. The Nazarene. It was heartbreaking."

"Heartbreaking?"

"Weren't you coming from Jerusalem?"

"And thereabouts."

"And you didn't hear about the clamor last weekend? When he arrived. And the uproar at his trial when all the fools wanted him crucified?"

"Tell me."

"We thought . . . ," Mary said.

"We thought he was the One," Cleophas interrupted, "you know? The Messiah. He did wondrous things. Curing people. And teaching kindness. Forgiveness. No matter what. But . . . but then he . . . pushed things too far. They say he did. They say he claimed he was . . . he was equal to God. Or something like that."

"That's why they killed him," Mary said. "Then they told the Romans he wanted to be made king. The priests made that up. Because of the Messiah being . . . well, like David. But he wasn't like that at all. But the Romans didn't want trouble. So they crucified him. That gentle, kind man. They nailed his hands and feet, and . . . ," she began to choke on her tears.

"She was there," Cleophas said, and put his arm around her shoulders. "Such hopes. But the Messiah's not supposed to be . . . to be degraded like that . . . not treated like a dog. The Holy One would never allow that."

"Why not?" the stranger asked.

The man and wife stopped and stood, unsure again. "Are you a Jew?" Cleophas asked.

"Of course," the big stranger smiled.

"Then you've been taught. The holy books say Elijah would come. That was John the Baptist. Then the Messiah would come, like Moses, and lead us out of bondage again. And like David, he'd make us a people again. Make all things right again."

"Like this Nazarene," the stranger said, "just healing, forgiving, bringing only peace."

"Yes." Mary's tears were running freely now, and her husband's were brimming.

"The holy books," the big stranger said. "You remember Job?"

"Of course," Cleophas replied, a bit insulted.

"But you don't remember, early on? Before Job's friends confused him? When he said, 'Naked came I out of my mother's womb, and naked shall I return thither. The Lord gave, and the Lord hath taken away; blessed be the name of the Lord.' You were willing to take the good parts—the healing, the forgiveness. But not the pain, not the cost of loving."

"But . . ."

"You've let the priests push aside the prophets. They goad you with fear onto the right road and then they brighten it with the promise to take away all pain, all sorrow. Instead of helping you make sense of it." He smiled at Mary. "Do you have children?"

"Four," she said.

"Were any of their births joyous?"

She hesitated. "When it was over."

"Exactly! Suffering, then joy. Neither one would have any meaning without the other."

They began to walk again, more slowly now. And the stranger led them through the Scriptures, quoting passage after passage that showed them how shallow and one-sided their ideas of the Messiah had been.

He reminded them of Isaiah's Messiah, "'There was nothing appealing about him, nothing to call for a second look. Despised, useless, a man who knew pain like his shadow. Shunned, reviled, dirt. But it was *our* pains he carried, *our* burdens, *our* disfigurements, whatever is wrong with *us*.'"

The husband and wife listened, fumbling to take it in as he went on and on. "'He was beaten, tortured, but he didn't say a word. A lamb to the slaughter. Silent. They trampled justice to take him away. Who could have guessed what was really happening? Slain for the sins of my people, buried with the wicked, even though he'd never harmed a soul or said one untrue word.'"

He quoted Zechariah as knowingly as if he had written it himself: "'Oh, then I'll rain down a torrent of grace and peace on the house of David and all in Jerusalem. They'll look at Me whom they pierced. They will mourn for Him as for an only child.' As you were mourning."

Without realizing, they had walked into the village, where the oil lamps were beginning to puncture the darkness. The inn was just ahead.

"Well, then," the stranger smiled broadly again. "Here we are. I'll be going on."

"It's late," Mary said, a hint of concern in her voice. "It's too dangerous on the road in the dark. By yourself."

"Have you eaten?" Cleophas asked.

"Not in some time," the stranger answered.

"Then come in for a bite," Mary urged. "And stay the night. Not expensive. We checked. And if you haven't enough . . ."

So they went in and found places in the noisy tavern. When their food came, the stranger reached bread from the basket and said: "*Barukh attah Adonai Elohenu Melek.*... Blessed are you, O Lord our God, King of Ages, who brings forth bread from earth." He looked at his two friends, and tore the bread in half, handing them the pieces, taking none himself.

They had followed him a very long time. At the wedding he had transformed water into wine. Out in the stony wilderness, he had—somehow—fed thousands with no more than a couple of loaves. They had heard the Twelve whispering about his mystical farewell meal with them the night before that horrible day.

And at that instant, they knew him. In the breaking of the bread.

Then, suddenly, he was no longer there. And yet . . .

Thomas the Twin had not been with them that first time. When they told him they'd seen Jesus, his first reaction was fury. A joke like that was heartless. Obscene. The more they tried to persuade him, the stronger his resistance grew. They were all as crazy as the devil-woman. "Just stop it!" he finally shouted. "When I put my finger into his wrists and my hand into his chest, then I'll believe the rotten lot of you!"

A week later, Jesus met Thomas's challenge.

They were huddled together in the upper room, all eleven of the ones still faithful. Each in his own way. There'd been no news of a pogrom from the Temple. On the other hand, there'd been no news of a reprieve and no end of rumors.

Then, from nowhere, Jesus stood there among them. Solid, impenetrable, real. Even if the door to the stairs was barred. Right next to where Thomas hunched at the end of a couch.

"Shalom," he said softly. "I missed you, Thomas."

Thomas shuddered. Terrified. Confounded. "Oh, my God!" he gasped.

Jesus hugged the poor man in his big arms and stroked his back. "Oh, Thomas," he said. "I know it's hard." Then he held him at arm's length, let him go. He held out his wrists. "Put your finger into the scars, Thomas. Don't ever be afraid again."

But Thomas couldn't. And there was no need to.

> Now Jesus did many other signs in the presence of his disciples, which are not written in this book. But these are written so that you may come to believe that Jesus is the

Messiah, the Son of God, and that through believing you may have life in his name. (JN 20:30-31)

Puzzling Moments

What "Really" Happened

This is THE question. As St. Paul rightly insisted, "If Christ has not been raised, then our proclamation has been in vain and your faith has been in vain" (1 COR 15:14).

The spear negates resuscitation. Beyond argument, the early Christians—and the four authors of the Gospels—believed (to the death) Jesus had actually, really, reentered time after having definitively left it. This was no "replacement," like Eastern transmigration of souls and reincarnation. According to the eyewitnesses, this is the original body, "somehow" transformed.

Nor are these experiences "psychogenic projections" or "virtual presences" like Princess Leia or "out-of-body experiences" widely testified to by near-dead patients witnessing "a heavenly light." The Jesus the disciples encountered was radically different from the visions of the book of Revelation and even from St. Paul's meeting the risen Christ as a blinding light: "He heard a voice but saw no one" (ACTS 9:7).

But, like Thomas, we need tactile *proof.* Even though nearly all we claim to "know for a fact"—from physics, chemistry, biology, history, psychology—are convictions for which we have nothing even approaching "compelling evidence." All of it we take on the testimony of experts who seem to have no motive to deceive us.

It comes as some surprise that so few realize how pitifully little of what we "are sure of" comes from firsthand experience or from personal gathering of evidence, analyzing, organizing, concluding, critiquing. Almost all we know comes predigested from equally dependent parents, teachers, peers, and most effectively now from the lifelong Electronic Babysitter. Most of what any of us knows is based on trust in what others claim to have observed or reasoned to without any motive to deceive. I've never been to China or Alpha Centauri, never pinched an atom or cupped a neutrino in my palm like a captured firefly. Most of what I accept as true is based (at last implicitly) on the assumption that most people tell the truth.

The reason the resurrection begs for more than secondhand, academic knowledge is that accepting it as true is *more* than accepting the volatility of physical objects that seem inert and solid. The truth of the resurrection opens a dimension to human life and meaning and purpose no empirical knowledge can handle. It means accepting that death does not annihilate our accomplishments, that what seem to be our time/space cramped lives echo *infinitely*. It means that an afterlife is not just wishful thinking.

Basic question: Did the appearances "cause" the faith or did the profound desire that it be true "validate" imaginative creation of the appearances? Big difference between, on the one hand, fabricating concrete details (Thomas's probing—or the "special effects" at the crucifixion) to "solidify" the power of their experience and, on the other, falsifying their experience entirely.

The first uses embellishing details we all presume in everyday practice with metaphors and symbols, trying to capture an entity that is truly there—like love, courage, learning—in a heart, a medal, a diploma. Throwing clothes on an Invisible Man who is actually *there*. The other practice is asking belief in an Invisible Man most critical people know *isn't* there.

Does anyone—even the most prestigious scriptural expert—wrestle with the staggering difficulty the first witnesses to these unprecedented events faced in trying to put into words what defied reason? Was he physical or not? "All I know is that he was *real*, dammit!" Ask a couple at their fiftieth wedding anniversary why they stayed together for so long.

Being like does not equal being the same. Analogies are attempts to explain some reality one doesn't understand by comparison to something one does understand: "War is hell; Alfie is a pig; My heart's on fire." By definition, analogies are *always* inadequate: God is not an old man on a throne; an atom is not a tiny solar system; red is not the burn of cinnamon on your tongue. But the metaphors are better than nothing. So when people try to lessen the blockage between "heavenly" and "body," they are not equating the two referents. One can readily shoot holes in any conjunction of the mystifying, paintless image of a crucified corpse on the Shroud of Turin with the ghostly images "imprinted" on Hiroshima walls by fissioned bodies. But it helps lessen both our disturbing doubts and our arrogant certainties.

However, I'd suggest there just might be a tunnel under disbelief in near-universal acceptance of *Star Trek*'s teletransportation ("Beam us up, Scotty!") The viewer suspends disbelief and simply accepts that atoms and molecules of solid flesh move through space—and the heavily fortified skins of spaceships—and reassemble in proper alignment. Still separate, and not a rearrangement of Kirk and Spock. This is based on the scientific "belief" that if (*per impossible*) I could conform the molecules in my hand to those in the desk I'm tapping away on, my hand could conceivably pass right through it. That's not arcane theology. Just hard science.

Whatever limits we, after two thousand years of probing, demand for the meaning of "reality" of the risen Jesus, a great many of those witnesses believed the presence real enough to die for.

What defies comprehension is that brilliant men and women today, who find no slightest hesitation in yielding to the unimaginably large universe once compacted into a singularity—a dot "smaller than a point in mathematics"—could doubt that "some unknown power," which conspired to invent life in the first place, would be blocked from giving life back to a dead man.

It is equally puzzling that even believers who accept the incarnation—that God "smallened" himself into the carpenter, Jesus—would be helpless to bring him *back* to life. Both the original witnesses and believers well into the second and third centuries—and still today—believe that Mary Magdalene at the empty tomb saw the same incarnate God she had loved in life.

Unlike the annunciation, if someone had a camera at the tomb, Jesus *would* have been captured on film. This was no "symbol." (Aquinas's hymn says: *Dat panis caelicus figuris terminum*—"This heavenly bread was the ending of mere symbols.")

Consider all the eviscerating half-truths that try to gut the event: "Jesus rose only in our minds and hearts, our lives and dreams," like the vase of Grandma's ashes on the mantelpiece. No. This event declares unambivalently that the God of Creation, the God of Job, the God of Forever is now and always physically present to us. Not just in the way God has always been *ehyeh asher ehyeh,* the pool of existence out of whom everything with "is" draws its "is." God is now focused, self-trapped, embodied into our midst. *Emmanuel.*

Malle, the half-wit mystic in H. F. M. Prescott's great novel *The Man on a Donkey*, captures it: "He came stilly as rain, and even now cometh into the darkness of our bellies—God in a bit of bread, to bring morning into our souls. *There* is news!"

The absolute rock-bottom issue comes to: How large are you personally willing to "allow" reality to be?

Bodily Resurrection

What could possibly constitute a risen body? A material immateriality?

If "where" God is has nothing to do with time and space (it anteceded them), "where" did the physical bodies of Jesus and

Mary go at the ascension and assumption? There was no "space" for them "there." (See how the more you know, the less certain you can be?)

The Gospels take pains to assert *both* the palpable physical presence (eating, Thomas's probing the scars) *and* strange new properties that defy natural laws (appearing inside a locked room, disappearing from the sight of the Emmaus travelers, rising "up" into heaven).

Some assert that it was a "pneumatic body" or an "incorporeal body." (Gk: *pneuma* = "spirit," lessened in ordinary speech to nothing more than "gas.") But the unredeemed part of me responds, "Whatever the hell *that* means!" Yet again we come up flat against a conjunction that is either an out-and-out impossibility or a paradox, a matter of what physicists call complementarity, viz., the solid/immaterial electron.

To get nitty-gritty: If Magdalene had a camera when she encountered "the gardener," would he have made a real pattern not only on her retinas but on an utterly indifferent film? If Richard Dawkins had been there, would he have seen Jesus? *Could* he have? Or would the resistances he'd built up over a lifetime negate even the possibility? Can the Grand Dragon of the Ku Klux Klan admire the basic decency of Martin Luther King, Jr., and Nelson Mandela? Could Ptolemy have accepted Copernicus? Or Galileo? Much less Heisenberg?

Gerald O'Collins writes: "Most New Testament scholars would be reluctant to assert that the risen Christ became present in such a way that neutral (or even hostile) spectators could have observed him in an ordinary 'physical' fashion." Note first the caution: "reluctant." They don't want to be trapped in an assertion or denial when they feel the evidence can't support either.

Therefore, accepting the risen Christ is "special." Put one way, it requires a suspension of *dis*belief; put positively, it requires "enhanced vision." The "grace" of faith. Apprehension of the risen

Christ (then and now) requires a recognition deeper than normal cognition or visual perception. Why can't puritans comprehend jokes? Or passion? During his life, what did the disciples see in Jesus Pharisees *couldn't*? Not ill will but gut prejudice against the *possibility*.

Note also that at first no one recognizes Jesus. How could they? No matter what we ourselves have heard and accepted since childhood about resurrection, it would take more than mindless gullibility merely to smile when a friend says, "While I was in the checkout at Walgreens today, I saw Elvis Presley in the next aisle."

Not only was resurrection unheard of. He was *transformed*! He had "gone back into" a totally *new* way of *existing*. (If you console anyone at a wake, you've already admitted that has to be possible.)

Eyes of Faith

Their universal resistance to the reality of the risen Jesus shows the concept of resurrection is not clearly, *a priori* "self-evident," like the truths of the *Declaration* that all humans are equal or your certainty that I had two parents, one male and one female, or the conclusion that, if the streets are dry, it's not raining.

Faith does not mean smothering our rational intelligence, or resting belief solely either on the Church or Bible or our parents' faith. Much less an absolutely stupid "blind leap in the dark." But it does require that we resist the inflexible *tyranny* of logic bred into us by almost exclusively left-brain, empirical schooling and misunderstanding of "hard science," which—contrary to most people's belief—humbly and admirably claims not dogma but high degrees of probability.

Believers are like actors during a play, suspending a gut awareness that one thousand people are out there in the dark witnessing their agony, lust, degradation—purposely, so they can inhabit a character whom in real life they would detest. It means lowering the instinctive "guard-up" minds we work with all day in a world where everybody's a liar. (It's called paranoia.)

Some objectors to the reality of the resurrection claim it would be more acceptable if testimony came from indifferent or (even better) hostile witnesses. The objection is truly silly. Or else merely uninformed, unaware that not a single witness to the resurrection got "taken in."

How could someone give *reliable* testimony to a resurrected Jesus who still remained neutral about the possibility of resurrection? Such objectors ignore the fact that the Apostle Thomas was manifestly a disbeliever and that St. Paul was not only a disbeliever but a rabid persecutor of believers. Jesus' reappearance utterly defied what anybody found acceptable.

When Einstein claimed God doesn't play dice with the universe, Niels Bohr reportedly said, "Albert, don't tell God what he can do."

An absolute precondition for even setting out to find the truth of the resurrection is at least some acceptance of the *possibility* of a transcendent dimension to reality. The first sentence of Carl Sagan's monumental *Cosmos* claims: "The cosmos is all there is, and all there ever was, and all there ever will be." Hardly the open mind one might expect from a brilliant thinker setting out on an honest quest: denying even the possibility of the Quarry.

It is thus utterly impossible to grasp the "purely historical Jesus" without any "taint" of faith intruding on the evidence. Anybody who reported it to be true, with no access to a Geiger counter or high-speed film, believed it. Each one was *part* of the evidence, just like two golden jubilarians attesting to their lifelong love. Even physics is now forced to accept that the one viewing the evidence has to "get into the cosmic dance and move with it" in order to understand it fully. What's more, there are some questions empirical science simply cannot handle. For instance, it will never answer the question of when a human fetus becomes an undeniable *person*. Nor validate love, or detect truth, or drive a nail into mercury without it falling apart.

This is not to go back to the lobotomizing "faith" that held the "Catholic truths" to be unassailable and thus every deduction from them equally "infallible." On the other hand, it doesn't yield to the alternate infallibility of the human mind that supposedly validates geniuses like Thomas Jefferson snipping out only the Bible verses that suited his assertions about the limits of reality and Carl Sagan's denial of even the possibility of any such realities.

The absolute rock-bottom issue comes to: How large are you personally willing to "allow" reality to be?

Emmaus

Those of us over fifty remember the "Kennedy Weekend," when the war hero who embodied all we thought good about ourselves was shattered by a pasty-faced nobody. Then he in turn was shot by the operator of a strip-joint. It was unthinkable. Unbearable. Obscene. The whole world seemed to come to a complete, weak-in-the-knees standstill. That's what the two travelers on the road to Emmaus carried with them. Desolation. Nor did they recognize Jesus either. Even though their shattered souls desperately *wanted* him back!

At this point, as often in writing these pages, I was pulled up short, despite all those mind-numbing years in theology and fifty years since. Why did they "recognize him in the breaking of the bread"? There is at least no mention of anyone but the Twelve at the Last Supper—even though it's highly unlikely men would do women's work.

But this is one of the most elegantly *crafted* stories in the Gospels. Managed. And it clearly follows the outline of the liturgy, then and still. The Emmaus meal even uses the identical Greek verbs from the Last Supper. Whether this couple was at the supper, or they had heard about it, it is beyond argument that such an interpretation by his readers is what Luke intended.

This tidy story is the outline of Eucharist: Scripture, explanation, breaking bread.

Elements to Ponder

Unworthiness

Can we be humble enough to allow our own exaltation? That each of us—through no fault or merit of our own—is worth the crucifixion? Can we accept the staggering fact that the resurrection is nothing less than exalting the whole human race—and the universe itself—into the life of God? Gerald O'Collins, S.J., writes: "The divine presence in the material world, initiated at the creation and dramatically enhanced by the incarnation, is now being consummated by the resurrection and its universal promise."

Humble enough to accept the task of being the salt of the earth?

Beyond Justice and Morality

The priest and the levite in the parable of the Good Samaritan did nothing unjust or immoral. They merely walked by, minding their own business, which many believe is a Christian virtue. But they clearly did not qualify as "Christian." The reason was that they were unkind.

One clear example of the warp-thrust leap of Christianity beyond justice occurs in Victor Hugo's *Les Miserables*. When the gendarmes return Jean Valjean, Bishop Bienvenu had every right—in justice—not only to the return of his stolen silverware but to some kind of punitive damages for the betrayal of his hospitality and trust. Instead:

"Ah! here you are!" he exclaimed, looking at Jean Valjean. "I am glad to see you. Well, but how is this? I gave you the candlesticks too, which are of silver like the rest, and for which you can certainly get two hundred francs. Why did you not carry them away with your forks and spoons?"

That is well beyond justice. That's the father of the prodigal, the carpenter with the adulteress, and with the woman known as a sinner in the town, and with the Samaritan woman at the well, and with the kindly rebel, and with the cowering first-chosen, and his first deputy, Peter. And with all the wastrels and ne'er-do-wells and hotheads and sloths and hemorrhoids we spy along our own road to Jericho.

"Welcome! Even if you're unbaptized, divorced, gay, confused, sinful, lost. So are we. You're welcome here."

Thomas

Not a single one of the apostles the Son of God purposely chose was an *ideal* disciple. Just the *usual* disciple. Fumbly as Simon Peter, romantic as John, self-protective as Judas, naive as Nathaniel, and in general as colorless and ill defined as all the others. But the one apostle most Christians with the slightest sophistication resonate to is Thomas, the Skeptic.

He was a no-nonsense inspector general, time-study man, chess player, a realist, not a poet. The last time he'd eaten with Jesus, Jesus had said he was leaving for a while, but some day they'd follow. The others just sat there, nodding, as if they had even the slightest notion. But Thomas couldn't harness his literalist itch. "All right," he'd said. "*Where?*" And Jesus had said that he—Jesus—*was* the way. Which wasn't the slightest bit easier to swallow than the first bit. All these roundabouts and curves, these parables instead of a flat-out, satisfying answer.

The key to honest learning is honest doubt. And there isn't an honest man or woman who'd deny the offer Thomas had.

The Deepest Question

How could this utter failure have convinced these so-stubborn, so-resistant monotheists that he was God? How did panicky cowards become fearless martyrs? Why did this one Hebrew breakaway sect succeed, worldwide—not John's, not Essenes?

It had to be something *staggering*.

And here's the kicker: Despite indescribable infamies from without and even worse from within, the enterprise begun by this handful of losers has lasted two thousand years. Miraculous!

Never say "Impossible" to God.